CAMBRIDGE LIBRARY COLLECTION

Books of enduring scholarly value

Literary Studies

This series provides a high-quality selection of early printings of literary works, textual editions, anthologies and literary criticism which are of lasting scholarly interest. Ranging from Old English to Shakespeare to early twentieth-century work from around the world, these books offer a valuable resource for scholars in reception history, textual editing, and literary studies.

Ruskin and the English Lakes

John Ruskin (1819–1900), the influential Victorian art critic and social theorist, lived in the Lake District for nearly 30 years. This biographical study, first published in 1901, focuses on the significance of the region in Ruskin's life and art. It begins with his first visit as a five-year-old, when he became "a dedicated spirit' to the beauty and the wonders of Nature', and ends with accounts of his funeral and memorial at Coniston. It describes his commitment to the local people and their traditional crafts, and his relationship with the poet Wordsworth. The author, H. D. Rawnsley (1851–1920), was a clergyman, conservationist and keen art lover based in the Lake District who had been personally tutored by Ruskin and who was one of the founders, in 1884, of the heritage organisation that became the National Trust.

T0371577

Ruskin and the English Lakes

H.D. Rawnsley

CAMBRIDGE
UNIVERSITY PRESS

CAMBRIDGE UNIVERSITY PRESS

Cambridge, New York, Melbourne, Madrid, Cape Town,
Singapore, São Paolo, Delhi, Tokyo, Mexico City

Published in the United States of America by Cambridge University Press, New York

www.cambridge.org
Information on this title: www.cambridge.org/9781108036009

© in this compilation Cambridge University Press 2011

This edition first published 1901
This digitally printed version 2011

ISBN 978-1-108-03600-9 Paperback

RUSKIN AND THE ENGLISH LAKES

From Photo. by Barraud.

JOHN RUSKIN, AETAT 63.

Ruskin and the English Lakes

By the Rev.

H. D. Rawnsley

Hon. Canon of Carlisle
Author of "Literary Associations of the English Lakes"
"Life and Nature at the English Lakes"
"Memories of the Tennysons"
etc., etc.

Glasgow

James MacLehose and Sons

Publishers to the University

1901

GLASGOW: PRINTED AT THE UNIVERSITY PRESS
BY ROBERT MACLEHOSE AND CO.

To

MARION TWELVES

A DEVOTED FRIEND AND DISCIPLE OF
JOHN RUSKIN, WHO HAS EARNESTLY TRIED TO
CARRY INTO DAILY PRACTICE THE
SPIRIT AND PRINCIPLES OF
HIS TEACHING

PREFATORY NOTE

I wish to thank Mr. W. S. Collingwood for the great help his Biography and his Notes in the Catalogue of the Coniston Exhibition afforded me, and Mr. George Allen for his courtesy in allowing me to quote sundry passages in the works of John Ruskin. The hymns sung at Ruskin's funeral and the poems written on the occasion of his death will be found in the Appendix.

H. D. R.

CROSTHWAITE VICARAGE,
September, 1901.

CONTENTS

CHAPTER I.

CHAPTER VI.

CHAPTER VII.

CHAPTER VIII.

CHAPTER IX.

CHAPTER X.

LIST OF ILLUSTRATIONS

CHAPTER I.

RUSKIN AND THE ENGLISH LAKES.

RUSKIN first saw the English Lakes in 1824, when as a child of five and a half years old he journeyed in Mr. Telford's comfortable travelling coach with his mother and father and the Scotch nurse Anne from London to the north.

What wine business the firm of Ruskin, Telford & Domecq hoped to do at Keswick I know not, but if it was to start the son of the younger partner in his own business in life, the visit was eventful and well rewarded. For it was on this visit that the little lad, scrambling about at Friars' Crag in charge of his nurse, felt the scene so appeal to him as to make him from that hour 'a dedicated spirit' to the beauty and the wonders of Nature.

Writing of that visit long years after, Ruskin said: "The first thing that I remember as an event in life was being taken by my nurse to the brow of Friars' Crag, Derwentwater. The intense joy mingled with awe that I had in looking through the hollows in the mossy roots over the crag into the dark lake has associated itself more or less with all twining roots of trees ever since." How deep was the impression made upon his child mind by that visit to Friars' Crag we know from a passage in *Praeterita*, where speaking of another lad he says, "With their son five years old, just at the age when I look back to the creation of the world for *me* in Friars' Crag, Derwentwater."

Two years later, in 1826, the seven-year-old boy-poet,—for in this year he composed his first poem,—found himself again sitting on his clothes-box between his mother and father, driving for his summer tour to Perth, and for the second time he visited the English Lakes.

What he saw we know not, though it is pretty certain that he would make some notes in childish fashion in his diary. In 1830, at eleven years old, observer now of men and Nature, he again comes to Windermere, Keswick, Ullswater, and Coniston. The careful record of that journey which he and his sister-cousin Mary kept between them is preserved, and a poem in four books, begun the 28th of November, 1830, and finished 11th January, 1832, entitled the *Iteriad*, gives us in rhyme the facts of the diary.

That journey to the Lakes, so far as its strength of impression went, was perhaps the most remarkable of any he ever took. He had already felt the added pleasure that human association gives to scenery. His parents seem to have called out his early passion for romance in localities, by judiciously putting into his hands the books or tales embodying the spirit of the scenes. Readers of *Praeterita* will remember how Ruskin more than half a century after, writing of that *Iteriad* journey, says,—"There was one district however—that of the Cumberland lakes, which needed no charm of association to deepen the appeal to realities. I have said somewhere that my first memory in life was Friars' Crag on Derwentwater: meaning I suppose my first memory of things afterwards chiefly precious to me : at all events I knew Keswick before I knew Perth, and after the Perth days were ended my mother and I stayed either there at the Royal Oak, or at Low-wood Inn, or at

Coniston, Waterhead, while my father went on his business journeys to Whitehaven, Lancaster, Newcastle, and other northern towns."

"The inn at Coniston was then actually at the upper end of the lake, the road from Ambleside to the village passing just between it and the water, and the view of the long reach of lake with its softly wooded lateral hills had for my father a tender charm with which he afterwards regarded the lakes of Italy. Low-wood Inn also was then little more than a country cottage, and Ambleside a rural village : and the absolute peace and bliss which anyone who cared for grassy hills and for sweet waters might find at every footstep, and every turn of the crag or bend of bay was totally unlike anything I ever saw or read of elsewhere."

The more one reads the boy's poem the more one is struck with the way in which that little lad of eleven saw and noted what was really best worth seeing in the district. The main features of the scene of Derwentwater and its isles from Latrigg, the summit of Skiddaw, with its loose shales and its bitter wind-blown ridge, are faithfully described, though he was in error in taking a buzzard for an eagle. We almost feel the boy's delight

when at the descent to Troutbeck Bridge in
a thrice happy moment,

> "Windermere's sheet
> In its bright sylvan beauty lay stretched at his feet."

He did not know it, but the same little
stream that crosses the road and sings its way
to the lake shore near Low-wood, by which
Wordsworth and his sister rested and rejoiced
when they first made their walking tour to
the lakes at the beginning of the century,
attracted his eyes and charmed his heart:

> "So fair was the wood on which now we did gaze,
>   Admiring the flowery moss-carpeted maze,
>   And there a small streamlet with verdant banks sung."

He notes the poplars—alas, long since
fallen—at Low-wood, the blue of the Langdale Pikes and Scafell, the glory of the
sunset as seen from Low-wood. At Grasmere, Butterlip How as a vantage ground
attracts him. He sees the rills innumerable
that are such a feature of the western side
of the vale. This same fellside jewelry of
streams he notes on Helvellyn: "Helvellyn,
Helvellyn that mountain of might." He
speaks of these streamlets on the flanks of
Helvellyn like "threads of pure silver which
hung from the sky." The "heathy swells,"
which afterwards Matthew Arnold immortalised

on the Armboth fells, do not escape him. The famous view of Derwentwater from the hill below the moor, which made Gray the poet almost wish to turn back and stay a little longer at Keswick, impresses him deeply. Friars' Crag he revisits without his nurse, and notices the way the boats, as they swing at their anchorage, divide the ripples. He observes the net-like weaving of the fir, oak, and elm roots above the rocks at Friars' Crag. He is indignant that the washerwomen of Keswick should disfigure the scene by turning Friars' Crag and its trees and their boughs into a drying ground for their linen. He loses his way in Cockshott, but climbs Castle Head. Its sun-wasted turf, its wind-blown knotted oak trees, its wild flowers, all these are remembered. He makes a point of seeing Southey, and does this by going to church at Crosthwaite, "as much for the poet as the preaching":

"His hair was no colour at all by the way,
  But half of't was black slightly scattered with grey,
  His eyes were as black as a coal, but in turning
  They flashed—ay, as much as a coal does in burning;
  His nose in the midst took a small outward bend,
  Rather hooked like an eagle's and sharp at the end."

The boy's eyes miss nothing. Up Borrodale he sees the great Bowder, or "Bauta" stone, and at once compares its poised mass to a ship's keel. The sternness of Honister Crag strikes him; the swift goings on of a thunderstorm at Buttermere, where

"The plunge of foam
On the lake's swelling bosom was dazzlingly thrown,"

are chronicled. He returns by Patterdale and Kirkstone to Low-wood, evidently impressed by the beauty of the houses at Clappersgate and the Croft. Already his mind is busy with the question of how far houses add to or take away from wild mountain scenes, which he worked out afterwards in *The Poetry of Architecture*, by his essay on the Westmoreland cottage. He goes from Low-wood for an excusion to Coniston. He describes with curious accuracy the hobblety, clumsy, huge-oared boat at the Windermere ferry; thinks they charged too much for toll there, as they charged too much for the hotel bill at Coniston. But the rain comes on, a veritable "laker," the fells are lost in storm, still the young journal-maker cannot help noting how the ghylls foam down over the fell face up by Tilberthwaite, and what a sound of brooks is in the valley. As the carriage climbs back out of the vale for home and Low-wood, he gazes back upon the Coniston lake, is struck by the beauty of rain-cloud and mist-hidden shores, and notes the way in which

> " The mountains all mistily softened away
> Appeared like thin clouds at the dawn of the day,"

while

> " Darker and deeper in bolder relief,
> As nearer approaching and rising the chief,
> The mighty Old Man with his dark summit reft,
> Closing the prospect arose on the left."

It is not great poetry truly, but it shows accuracy in observation, and the boy's heart is full to overflowing, for " among these mountains he has felt the strength of his desire," and he concludes his long *Iteriad* with the lines :

> " Farewell to the lake, and farewell to the mountain,
> The tarn and the torrent, the fell and the fountain,
> To the deeps of the dell and the wood-shaded shore,
> Thou land of the mountain I see thee no more."

The Lakeland scenery ' haunted him like a passion' for the next seven years of his life. The streams he loved to track to their source, the hills he loved to climb to their utmost heights in Westmoreland and Cumberland, were a perpetual presence that disturbed

him as it had disturbed Wordsworth's boyhood before him with sense of something far
more deeply interfused :

> "Whose dwelling is the light of setting suns,
>   And the round ocean and the living air,
>   And the blue sky, and in the mind of man."

We find the boy-poet, after a two years'
absence from the mountains, pouring forth
the yearnings of his heart for mountain glory,
and turning not to the 'blue hills' that his
baby ears had heard sung, and his young
eyes had seen beyond the Tweed, nor to
the nobler heights and vaster solitudes of
Wales, but to the hills of Cumberland and
Westmoreland that should be his companions
unto the end.   He writes :

> "I weary for the fountain foaming,
>   For shady holme and hill,
> My mind is on the mountain roaming,
>   My spirit's voice is still.
>
> I weary for the woodland brook
>   That wanders thro' the vale,
> I weary for the heights that look
>   Adown upon the dale.
>
> The crags are lone on Coniston
>   And Glaramara's dell,
> And dreary on the mighty one,
>   The cloud-enwreathed Sca-fell.

Oh, what although the crags are stern,
    Their mighty peaks that sever,
Fresh flies the breeze on mountain fern,
    And free on mountain heather.

I long to tread the mountain head
    Above the valley swelling,
I long to feel the breezes sped
    From grey and gaunt Helvellyn.

.   .   .   .

There is a thrill of strange delight
    That passes quivering o'er me,
When blue hills rise upon the sight
    Like summer clouds before me."

That desire to see the hills rise in the distance remained with him into later life, and no matter how beautiful the wide-spread plain of sun and shadow might be, if it failed at its horizon line to give promise of blue hills, he could not feel the scene had an enduring interest for him.

The boy of fourteen who from the neighbourhood of mighty London with all its attraction for boy life could 'weary' for the lake and lakeland hills and streams was no ordinary boy. A gift of Rogers' *Italy* illustrated by Turner in the same year sent him wild with desire to see grander heights and deeper vales and more majestic rivers, but though with Turner's sketches and De Saussure's *Ascent of Mont*

Blanc in hand he went twice to the continent before he became a Christ Church undergraduate, his love of the English lakes remained unshaken, and we find him in 1837, in his first long-vacation, bound for the North with his father, and back again at Keswick.

Speaking of this period of his life in *Praeterita*, Ruskin tells us that in that northern tour and at Catterick Bridge, he felt for the last time that pure childish love of Nature which Wordsworth so idly takes for an intimation of Immortality.   "It is," he says, "a feeling only possible in youth, for all care, regret, or knowledge of evil destroys it, and it requires also the full sensibility, sensibility of nerve and blood, the conscious strength of heart and hope."

"In myself," he continues, "it has always been quite exclusively confined to *wild*, that is to say, wholly natural places, and especially to scenery animated by streams or by the sea."

Ruskin, after assuring us that in 1837 he finds himself, in his primal passion for wild nature, unchanged from that day when in his northern tour he stood by the stream side at Catterick Bridge, and saw east and west the rising of the hills that foretold the presence of the Yorkshire moors, goes on to insist on the

curious joy he felt in returning to the scenes
of his boyhood. " No boy could possibly have
been more excited than I was by seeing Italy
and the Alps, neither boy nor man ever knew
better the difference between a Cumberland
cottage and Venetian palace, or a Cumberland
stream and the Rhone. My very knowledge
of this difference will be found next year
expressing itself in the first bit of promising
literary work I ever did, but after all the furious
excitement and wild joy of the contrast, the
coming back to a Yorkshire streamside felt
like returning to Heaven."   He adds, "We
went on into well-known Cumberland, my
father took me up Scafell and Helvellyn with
a clever Keswick guide, who knew mineralogy,
Mr. Wright, and the summer passed beneficently
and peacefully."

I never pass Wright's grave beside the
resting-place of Jonathan Otley in the Crosthwaite Churchyard, without a kind of sense
that I owe him thanks I cannot pay for all
he did for his young undergraduate pupil on
the slopes of Scafell in 1837, and through
him to those of us who have listened to the
Master discourse on the wonders of crystal
growth and the beauty of agate and spar.

It was very well that Ruskin had seen Italy

before he came to Yorkshire and the English Lakes in 1837. For the contrast between the cottages of Westmoreland and Italy set him thinking upon a subject which half of his future life was to be spent in discoursing of, " The Architecture of the Nations of Europe considered in its Association with Natural Scenery and National Character."

I have sometimes thought that it was fortunate that on the woody promontories of Derwentwater there were at that time what he describes as " staring square-windowed flat-roofed gentlemen's seats of the lath and plaster mock-magnificent Regent's Park description," and that on the shores of Coniston Lake there stood in its old-world beauty the solid-chimneyed substantial hall and farmhouse in one, to which tradition has it Sir Philip Sidney came in days of yore. For the former made him think seriously of what kind of country house ought not to be builded at the English Lakes, and the latter as he sketched it gave him thoughts about chimney building in general as expressive of a nation's life, and of the extraordinary fitness and beauty of the chimneys of our Westmoreland and Cumberland farms and cottages.

Little enough did the young draughtsman, as he sketched Coniston Hall with a view to

illustrating 'A Chapter on Chimneys,' think
that that old building by the lake side should
be one day a principal feature in the view
from his study window at Brantwood.

It was a happy chance that he determined to
put down his notes of lakeland travel in the
form of a series of articles for Loudon's *Archi-*
tectural Magazine. It obliged him to use his
pencil.

One of the many sketches made in this summer, 'A Ruin at Ambleside,' has been reproduced in the Poems, and we can see the influence
of his teacher Prout in every line of it.

If one turns to the first serious piece of
Art criticism he attempted, in 'The Poetry
of Architecture,' one is much struck by the
precocity of his right judgment, as well as by
the originality of his treatment of the subject,
but one is more struck by the beauty of his
English. He had read his Bible and his
Johnson to some purpose ; and it was a happy
thing that writing under the *nom de plume* of
' Kata Phusin ' he should in so short a phrase
have foreshadowed his whole life's work.

His happiest hunting ground for the ideal
and idyllic mountain cottage appears to have
been Troutbeck and Scandale, and very fortunate it was that he came into the country

before the hand of modern improvement and
the cottage - built - by - contract business had
superseded such efforts of the dalesmen to meet
the needs of generation after generation by
alteration and addition to their farms and
cottages, as they themselves with the help of
village joiner and waller could effect. The
charm of the cottage of Westmoreland and
Cumberland was that it was lowly in its own
eyes, a natural product, a thing that had grown
up in perfect harmony with its surroundings,
strong to withstand the wear and tear of mountain storms, and glad to emphasise by the curl
of its living smoke-wreath the loneliness of its
solitude.

But I expect its chief charm in Ruskin's
eyes was that in all its characteristics it told
the nature of the men who dwelt therein.
Men of sturdy, enduring, self-dependent mind,
who cared little for show and hated all sham.
"The uncultivated mountaineer of Cumberland," says Ruskin, at the end of his chapter
on 'The Mountain Cottage,' "has no taste
and no idea of what architecture means. He
never thinks of what is right and what is
beautiful, but he builds what is most adapted
to his purpose and most easily erected ; by
suiting the building to the use of his own

life he gives it humility, and by raising it
with the nearest material adapts it to its
situation."

The prophet of the 'beauty of use, and
use of beauty' found at the age of eighteen
in our lakeland hills texts which he could
preach from all his life; and certainly laid
here in the summer tours of 1837 and the
following year, the foundation-stone of much
of his Art criticism.

Ruskin had seen, but he had not at this
date spoken with Wordsworth. One can
easily imagine after perusing Wordsworth's
guide to the scenery of the Lakes, and notably
his chapter on the cottages of the Lake
country, with what gladness the old Rydalian
bard would have welcomed in this younger
poet and prophet of the English Lakes so
staunch a supporter of his own views.

"These humble dwellings," says Wordsworth, "remind the contemplative spectator
of a production of Nature, and may (using
a strong expression) rather be said to have
grown than to have been erected; the houses
rise by an instinct of their own out of the
natural rock."

And again, "These dwellings, mostly built
of rough unhewn stone, are roofed with slates

which were rudely taken from the quarry before the present art of splitting them was understood, and are therefore rough and un-even in their surface, so that both the coverings and sides of the houses have furnished places of rest for the seeds of lichens, mosses, ferns, and flowers. Hence buildings which in their very form call to mind the processes of Nature, do thus, clothed in part with vegetable garb, appear to be received into the bosom of the living principle of things, as it acts and exists among the woods and fields, and by their colour and shape effectively direct the thought to that tranquil course of Nature and simplicity along which the humble-minded inhabitants have through so many generations been led."

On one matter, however, young Ruskin and the old poet would have agreed to dis-agree. Wordsworth loved the peculiar build of chimneys that came in with the Flemings, "square up hauf waay and round th' tother." He took care that the chimneys of Foxhow should be so builded. He saw "a pleasing harmony between a tall chimney of this circular form and the living column of smoke ascending through the still air." But, though Ruskin rejoiced in the serviceableness and solidity of the broad-based Lake country chimneys, and

the quaint way in which they were built out
on stone corbels at the end of the cottage
rooftrees, he disliked cylindrical chimneys,
because they put him in mind of ' glass-houses
and manufactories,' yet even he was won to
admit that when the cylindrical chimney was
broadly based, and the base carried right down
to the ground as in Coniston Hall, there was
a lightness and picturesqueness given to the
distant outline of the mass, which was fit
and pleasing.

He set seriously to work upon his notes
on The Poetry of Architecture as soon as he
returned in the October term to Oxford.   It
was probably for the sake of these essays
he came again to the Lakes in the following
summer of 1838.   How well in these tours
he got to know the heart of our hills and
dales, may be gathered from a letter written
to a friend from Oxford under date July
31, 1840.   "In Cumberland everybody climbs
Skiddaw, so of course you will if you can.
Ascend the following mountains also, Helvellyn, Causey Pike, Scawfell, Langdale Pikes,
Coniston Man, and the Pillar of Ennerdale.
Do not miss Helvellyn on any account, and
go up the Thirlmere side, descending to Patterdale if you like, but on no account ascending

from Patterdale.   I could tell you why if I
had room which I have not, so trust me.

"The other peaks are named in the order
of their claims to ascent.   I think very highly
of the view from Causey Pike.   The Pillar I
have not myself ascended, but I know so
many places from which it is seen that the
view must be very fine.   Take care and don't
break your legs or your nose on Scawfell,
he is an awkward fellow and you may stick
between his loose rocks like Gulliver in the
narrow bone."   He probably did not know
as he penned this letter that Robert Southey
always praised the view from Causey Pike,
but it is to be hoped that his friend, instead
of climbing the Pillar, took the advice of
some one who had so done and contented
himself with 'Green Gable' instead.

"When you are at Keswick," he continues,
"and inclined for a long walk, go up the
meadows behind Walla Crag till you get near
the top.   Keep straight on the top of the
crags towards the head of the lake, catching
the view of Derwentwater down the ravines
—which if it be not cloudy are the finest
things in the neighbourhood.   When you have
passed the top of the crag, keep to your right,
a little as if you wanted to get down to the

shore; and don't slip, for it is very smooth
and steep and once off you would either roll
into the lake or get a most disagreeable
bruising on a *debris* of crag at the bottom.
In a little while you will come to a cart-road,
follow it *up* to your left till you come to a
stone bridge. Sit down on the rocks above
it, or in the water if you like it better, and eat
your lunch, and when you have done it, look
about you, for of all the landscapes I ever
saw in my life, I think the view of Derwentwater and Skiddaw from that spot with the
bridge for a front object is the best piece of
composition. When you have rested go up
further still. The cart-road will take you over
the crags above Lodore, on which you may
sit and kick your heels a little longer, and
mind the ants, for they are very big. When
you have got down to the stream of Lodore,
you will get the view of the lake through
the chasm, a favourite bit of Southey's, and
very tolerable indeed.

"Then walk up to Watendlath and, when you
have seen the tarn, back to Lodore, and boat it
up to Keswick. I shall not tell you any more
because I know travellers always take their own
way whatever advice they get."

Ruskin's accurate remembrance of localities

and their features is seen in this letter.   In a
later letter he speaks of Catchedecam and Styhead and shews he had not then gained
scientific knowledge of our hill names.   He makes
one very curious mistake, which Sir Walter
Scott in his poem *The Bridal of Triermain*
had made before him, in miscalling Blencathra,
Glaramara.   He half recovers himself, for he
says, " There is another name which I forget,
but it is a noble hill, a glorious hill, an
Olympian mountain, but deuced boggy."

His love of mineralogy comes out in this
letter.   He asks if his friend as he came over
Styhead looked for garnets?   " There are
plenty of them by the side of the road.   Wastwater," he says, " unless on a very fine day, is a
very black hole, nothing of a lake ; but I have
seen more beautiful atmospheric effects on the
Screes above, than on any hills in the country."

As postscript to the former letter he speaks
very highly of his old guide, the geologist
Wright, and he shews that he knew his man,
for Wright, so tradition has it, was given
"to stretch it a laal bit," as Cumbrians say.
" Wright at Keswick knows more about the
country than any other guide ; but don't believe
all he tells you about anything but rocks."

Nine years went by before Ruskin's next visit

to the Lakes.   In the interval his father had
removed from Herne to Denmark Hill.   He
had travelled and studied much, and had become famous as the writer of *Modern Painters*,
the first volume of which appeared in the spring
of 1841, and the second in 1846.

Worn out by the labour of this second volume,
he returned from a tour to the Continent with
his parents in October of that year, refreshed in
body but not in mind, but was soon busy upon
work for the *Quarterly*.   He had been placed
by Lockhart upon the staff of that periodical,
and there is reason to believe that immensely
attracted to Lockhart by reason of Lockhart's
love for Sir Walter Scott, he was more attracted
by reason of his own admiration for Lockhart's
daughter.

The little, high foreheaded Charlotte Lockhart, so he tells us in *Praeterita*, had become to
him a Scottish fairy, a White Lady and witch
of the fatallest sort, but though he used to see
her sometimes at Lady Davy's he never could
contrive to come to any serious speech with her,
and at last with his usual wisdom in such
matters, went away into Cumberland to re-
commend himself to her by writing for *The
Quarterly Review*.   The book he undertook to
review was Lord Lindsay's *Christian Art*; the

place where he determined to write his review was Ambleside.

" I went," says he, " in the early Spring to the Salutation at Ambleside then (this was in 1847) yet a country village, and its inn a country inn. But there, whether it was the grilled salmon for breakfast or too prolonged reflection on the Celestial Hierarchies, I fell into a state of despondency till then unknown to me, of which I knew not the like till fourteen years afterwards. The whole morning was painfully spent in balancing phrases, and from my boat in the afternoons on Windermere it appeared to me that the water was leaden and the hills low."

How much of this despondency was owing to dyspepsia, and how much to love we know not, but it is clear that the Lake country in the spring of 1847 had no power to minister to a mind so diseased ; he went back to Leamington and the doctor stopped the grilled salmon and ordered salts and promenade. His parents, who knew of his love-sickness were, it seems, opposed to the idea of his offering Miss Lock-hart hand and heart, and, dutiful son as he was, to his own undoing he gave up hopes in that direction, and as obediently in the autumn of the same year proposed to and was accepted by that Fair Maid of Perth to whom he had some years before indited *The King of the Golden River*.

Whatever the English Lake District could do to give rest and tranquillity to a troubled soul, it did for him in the following year. On the 10th of April, 1848, Ruskin married, and the young couple seem to have come straight to Keswick to spend their honeymoon.

If beauty of form and colouring in woman's shape could have made him happy then no happier bridegrom ever entered Keswick Vale; but what Ruskin needed was intensely sympathetic and constantly patient companionship, and already would it appear that the cloud had fallen, already the rift within the lute prevented the harmony of Heaven on earth he had hoped for. It is sad reading that letter to Miss Mitford from Keswick on Good Friday of 1848. " I begin to feel," he writes, "that all the work I have been doing, and all the loves I have been cherishing, are ineffective and frivolous, and that the time for endurance has come rather than for meditation, and for hope rather than for happiness. Happy those whose hope, without this severe and tearful rending away of all props and stability of earthly enjoyment, has been fixed 'where the world ceases from troubling.'

Mine was not ; it was based on 'those pillars of earth ' which are 'astonished at his reproof.' I have however," he adds, "passed this week, very happily here We have a good clergyman Mr. Myers, and I am recovering trust and tranquillity."

I have sometimes wondered whether it was at this time that as he climbed the Keswick Hill he felt a sign vouchsafed to him from heaven, and knew that there was one who answereth prayer. Long years after when the late Master of Baliol was at Brantwood visiting him whom he wrote of as "the gentlest and most innocent of mankind, of great genius but inconsecutive," Ruskin, by way of illustrating his religious belief, told him the following story. "Once I had been very much excited by a letter which I had received from a friend, and so great was my passion that my nerves were shaken for a fortnight. On a dark and stormy day I walked up the hill west of Keswick, and as I walked a sign came to me from heaven. I was praying to be delivered from my burden when suddenly a streak of light appeared in the heavens. I walked on and the clouds gathered and the old frame of mind returned again, and I prayed and again I saw the light."

Be that as it may, it has been at Keswick in 1848 that he found rest for his soul. A year ago he had felt how powerless the hills and Windermere were to heal his sickness, and to give him hope and joy, but the hills round Derwentwater now, though their splendour made him feel almost with pain a yearning for the mightier Alpine sights and scenes, gave him something of their peace and calm.

He who had written of the mountains that they are 'as a great and noble architecture, first giving shelter, comfort, and rest,' realised here in the Keswick Vale that they in part fulfilled their mission; and we may believe that not in vain did he find some anodyne for sadness, and some tonic for his disappointments in that generosity, and tender loving-kindness of our Cumberland hills, where "the whole heart of Nature seems thirsting to give and still to give, shedding forth her everlasting beneficence with a profusion so patient, so passionate that our utmost observance and thankfulness are but at best neglect of her nobleness and apathy to her love."

CHAPTER II.

NINETEEN years passed before Ruskin again
saw the blue-grey hills of Westmoreland and the
white waters of our Cumberland lakes. He had
written *The Seven Lamps* and *The Stones of
Venice*, helped to inaugurate the Working Men's
College, given his lectures on the Political
Economy of Art at Manchester, and taken his
last tour abroad with his parents. As hermit in
the wilds of Savoy he had left Art for social
problems and the study of rock formation, he
had felt the blow of fatherlessness, had penned
The Crown of Wild Olive, *Kings' Treasuries
and Queens' Gardens*, had begun *Time and
Tide.* He had delivered the Rede Lecture at
Cambridge and a lecture on Modern Art before
the Royal Institute, and tired of the noise of
town, with his *Time and Tide* half written,
he came down in July of 1867 to Keswick.

A friend, one of the truest Ruskin had, tells me of a memorable day on the lake with the Professor during that visit.

He was staying at the hotel at Portinscale, and arranged for her to come over with her hostess to spend a long day with him on Derwentwater. "If there is one thing I can claim to be able to do," he said, "it is to guide you to all that is best worth seeing and caring for on this lake. I know every tree and stone upon its shores, and the colour of every shallow and the clear deeps of every pool." So saying, they embarked, and leaving the river mouth and its rustling reeds, coasted all down the quiet western shore, touching land here and there to see the particular beauty of this or that tree or rock, or to get this or that particular view, loitering here to get some effect of gleam upon the grassy bottom of the lake, or rowing there to see a special reflected light on ripple or in shallow, he talking all the time of the wonder and the glory round about them; sad sometimes, as it seemed in sheer perverseness; glad sometimes and hopeful when the talk of the rest was sad, but making all feel that the hours were too swift and the eventide come too soon.

Ruskin must have always had a weak spot in

his heart for Keswick. In 1845 he tells us how the thought faintly and intermittently haunted his mother and himself that a rose-covered cottage in the dells of Matlock or the Vale of Keswick might be nearer the heavenly world than all the majesty of Denmark Hill ; and ever there hung Turner's picture of Derwentwater upon the Denmark Hill wall to call him northward. He once told a neighbour of mine that when he first knew Keswick it was a place he thought too beautiful to live in,—and when in later years he paid a visit to an Oxford friend in Under-skiddaw he was constantly expressing his wonder and amaze at the extraordinary beauty of the grouping of the hills to the west, and his delight in the level valley plain between Derwentwater and Bassenthwaite as giving value to the mountain scenery.

But he appears to have come to the English Lakes when worn out with work, or in de-spondency of soul ; one is not surprised to find that the hills seemed now to wear for him the purple of mourning, and that there was sadness for him in the light of setting suns ; but the fun of him comes to the front, and he writes to his cousin, a rhymed letter about the 'hot muffins' and hasty lunch which

preceded his climb up Red Pike. He seems
to have been gaining health and spirits by
his Cumberland tour, when suddenly after a
short stay at Ambleside, symptoms of over-
strain set in, giddiness of brain, mistiness of
the eyes, and he is forbidden all work for a
time.

In 1870 Oxford honoured herself by making
him Slade Professor. In 1871 was published
the first number of *Fors Clavigera*, and in
the same spring his favourite cousin, Joan
Agnew, married Arthur Severn. The added
labour and the added loss did not make for
health, and while away at Matlock he caught
a chill from rising early to sketch a sprig of
St. George's flower, the wild rose, and was
brought near to the land of shadows. It was
while he was slowly recovering that all the
old strong love of the English Lake country
came over him. If only he could journey as
he had journeyed forty years ago from that
same hostel, where he was now an invalid,
to the shores of Coniston, he felt sure he
should recover him of his sickness. There
was by Coniston Lake a rough little ten acres
of moorland with a copse that ran steeply
down to the Lake shore. In perfect privacy,
hardly seen from the road that ran between

it and the lake, stood a rough-cast, sturdily
built Westmoreland cottage that had once
belonged to the Sandys family, and that had
sheltered Gerald Massey the poet, and Linton
the engraver. A house that had echoed to
the chant of Massey's lyrics, and the sound
of Linton's sonnets was fit place for a poet
to come to, a home where the engraver had
worked was the place par excellence for one
to inhabit, who loved engravings and knew
more than most about them, and lastly a
house where the printing press had been set
up to give to the world the yellow-backed
Republic, and to proclaim by its wall mottoes
that 'God and the People' were the supreme
care of the master of the house, was a home
well adapted to receive one who was with all
his fierce conservatism, as fierce a reformer
as we have had in our time, and as zealous
a lover of the people and of God.

This fellside dwelling, perfect in its solitude
and privacy, as it was beautiful in its prospect
across the lake to the Old Man and Wetherlam,
or northward to Waterhead, Yewdale, and
Raven Crags, was blessed with access to moorland walk or lakeside ramble. A tiny stream
came down from the fells to feed whatever
plant life should be set for it to nourish, or

make whatever mimic waterfall the master
should please. The circling copse beloved of
nesting birds, gave shelter to the squirrel in
summer and to the woodcock in winter.
Mosses covered the roadside walls, wild roses
and fern and honeysuckle made the hedges
sweet for all who came that way, and a boat
below in the rough harbour offered easy means
of passage to Waterhead, if legs were weary
or horses failed.

Beautiful at all hours of the day, the view
from the cottage window was full of wonder
when the light mist-veils of early morning rose
from off the bosom of the lake, and floating up
the western hills, left the sloping lawns and
woods of Coniston sunny-clear above the perfect mirror of the lake. But sunset was the
time most magical. Then the Coniston fells
rose purple against the gold and red-saffron
of the west, and while the woods and lawns
darkened into silver grey, the levels of the
lake drank in the glory of the sky and floated
amber from marge to marge. But the chief joy
of the steep wood—Brantwood, as the natives
call it—was its retirement and its quietude. He
once spoke of the way in which the little Beck
Levens emphasised the sense of solitude, as
one wandered by the lake shore beneath the

BRANTWOOD.

From Photo. by H. Bell.

house. For weary heart and tired brain, could thinker and student find a fitter place of refuge?

It was to such a vantage place of view, and such a poet's haunt and writer's home, that *Fors*, as he would have said, led the brain-tired and weary Slade Professor, who was slowly recovering from his severe illness in his Oxford rooms in 1871.

Ruskin heard that Brantwood was for sale; £1500 was the price that Linton asked him for the house and its fellside ground, and the Professor bought it without sight of it. He tells us in his seventh volume of *Fors Clavigera* that it was "a mere shed of rotten timber and loose stone," and that it had to be furnished and repaired. "For old acquaintance sake," he says, "I went to my father's upholsterer (instead of the country Coniston one as I ought), and had £5 charged me for a foot stool; the repairs also proving worse than the complete rebuilding; I got myself at last settled at my tea-table one summer evening, with my view of the lake, for a net £4000. I afterwards built a lodge, nearly as big as the house, for a married servant, and cut and terraced a kitchen out of the 'steep wood,' another two thousand transferring themselves

c

thus into 'utilities embodied in material objects'
—but these latter operations under my own
immediate direction, turning out approvable by
neighbours, and I imagine not unprofitable
as investment."

He travelled up North to see his new possession in September, 1871, came on to
Keswick, thence for a short tour in Scotland,
and back for a day or two to Coniston in
October.   In December of that year, the
fatherless man was motherless also.   Those
who were undergraduates at Oxford remember
well when the accustomed blue tie was laid
aside, and how the whole of one term a black
tie was worn in its stead.   It was well he had
made himself another home.   At Easter of the
following year, 1872, he bade adieu to Denmark Hill, and in September came for the first
time into residence at Brantwood.

He came to it a broken-hearted man.   Those
who have read of the desire of his affectionate
heart to give and still to give, and of the
absolute necessity of his being to be loved,
knew the reason ; but he must have found
quiet and rest and strength and peace of mind
beside Coniston water, for he was able to go on
with his work for Oxford and the world.

The master of Brantwood was re-elected

Slade Professor in 1873, and came with the swallow to his lakeland home to write one of his best lectures, *The Swallow*, for his May audience. In June he was back in his study above the mere, and spent his first Long Vacation in the Coniston Vale. This time the Val D'Arno was in mind, and the work of Nicholas the Pisan was the subject of his pen. He does not appear to have spent more than a few weeks of the spring of 1874 at the lakes; he was away upon the Continent; Rome, Sicily, Assisi, Lucca, Switzerland, and the Jura charmed him, but he was continually back at Brantwood in thought. Tender little regrets at absence and desires to be at his own 'steep woodland' home are expressed in the correspondence with his devoted friend—I was going to write lover—at the Thwaite, Miss Susie Beever. Throughout the whole of this serio-playful and deeply-touching correspondence of lovers in old age, his wearying to be back at Brantwood makes itself felt. "I often think of you and Coniston and Brantwood—oh dear, I wish I were at Brantwood again." "Such moonlight here to-night (he is writing from Venice), but nothing to what it is at Coniston." "I am very well and sadly longing for Brantwood." "I trust very earnestly to be

safe in the shelter of my own woodside by the
end of October." "I made a little sketch of
the lake from above Waterhead, which goes
everywhere with me." Such sentences scattered
throughout a correspondence between 1874 and
1879 shew where his heart was.

That correspondence shews more.   It shews
how the deep human sympathy that in his
loneliness and pain he found to be his constant
neighbour at the Thwaite, strengthened and
refreshed him in his need, "when other friendship was failing and other loving mere folly."

"What one really wants," he writes from
Assisi, "I believe the only true restorative is
the natural one, the actual presence of one's
'helpmeet.' The far worse than absence of
mine reverses all the rest, and what is worse,
destroys one's power of receiving from others
or giving. How much love of mine have *others*
lost because that poor sick child would not
have the part of love that belonged to *her*."

In May of 1875 'that poor sick child' died,
and the more I read of the letters in *Hortus
Inclusus* the more I think I perceive how by
good providence it came to pass that the warm
admiration and affection of the ladies of the
Thwaite, and especially of Miss Susie Beever,
became to him the support and stay of his

declining years and the spur to his later efforts
and their hope.   It was of the greatest possible
good for him that Miss Susie undertook in
1874 the compilation of *Frondes Agrestes*.   It
entailed a correspondence full of delightful
sincerity and tender and true affection.   There
has seldom been such carrying on of the
child heart into age with all its innocent freshness and enthusiasm, as is manifest in the
lady's letters.   Seldom such understanding
hero-worship and helpful sympathy as was
shewn by these friends and neighbours, who at
so critical a time were raised up to him.

Ruskin writes in the preface to *Hortus
Inclusus* :

"They were types of perfect womanhood in
its constant happiness.   Queens alike of their
own hearts and of a Paradise in which they
knew the names and sympathised with the
spirits of every living creature that God had
made to play therein, or to blossom in its sunshine or shade. . . . Mary and Susie alike in
benevolence, serenity, and practical judgment
were yet widely different, nay almost contrary
in tone and impulse of intellect.   Both of them
capable of understanding whatever brain should
know, the elder was yet chiefly interested in the
course of immediate English business policy

and progressive science, while Susie lived an
aerial enchanted life, possessing all the highest
joys of imagination while she yielded to none of
its deceits, sicknesses, or crosses.   She saw and
felt and believed all good as it had been and
was to be in the reality and eternity of its good-
ness with the acceptance and hope of a child.
The least things were treasures to her and her
moments fuller of joy than some people's days."

As for the tender kindnesses, the little
presents, the tokens of continually thoughtful
friendship, that passed from Brantwood to the
Thwaite, and *vice versa*, the letters are a full
chronicle of these.   Now Ruskin will send a
Turner sketch or series of drawings to be gazed
upon, or a piece of crystal or pure gold for the
delight of their eyes.   Now Miss Beever will
dispatch a tuft of cranberries to be planted on
the moor, or some plant of rare interest for him
to study for his *Proserpina*, now a peacock's
feather, or a sketch of some bird's wing and
breast, which Ruskin, as he thanks her for sight
of, will describe thus, " The glory of velvet and
silk, and cloud and light, and black and tan and
gold, and golden sand and dark trees, and
purple shadows and mosses, and mists and night,
and starlight, woods and hills, and dells and
deeps, and every mystery of Heaven and its

fingerwork is in these little birds' backs and
wings.   I am so grateful.   All love and joy to
you, and wings to fly with and bird's heart to
comfort, and mine, be to you for the coming
year."   Then there were, too, little dainties
that passed very prettily from the Thwaite to
the Wood and from the Wood to the Thwaite in
times of illness.   Ruskin hears of Miss Beever
being unwell and orders his wine merchant to
send a case of his best champagne.   Miss
Beever learns that the Professor is ill, and aspa-
ragus or oysters, or some particularly delectable
currant jelly is forthwith dispatched.   The
Thwaite afternoon tea was an institution, and
the too seductive tea-cakes sometimes made
the Professor wander in Arabian deserts and
dodge hostile tribes round the Pyramids all
night.   He was never unwilling to dare the
venture again, and for real joy of the welcome
that awaited him, and the flow of soul that was
sure, would risk the nightmare.

1874 and 1875 were years of deep sorrow for
him, but he had his compensations.   It was not
only that he was now happy in the sincerest
friendship of the ladies of the Thwaite, and in
the pleasant neighbourhood of such kindly
people as the Victor Marshalls of Coniston,
he had during his second term of three years

as Slade Professor got in a quite astonishing manner at the heart of the undergraduate. One looks back as one writes these words to the crowded audiences at his Oxford lectures, to the delightful breakfasts of his young disciples with the Master at Corpus, to the new experiences, with their fruit for life, of being roadmakers for the Hinksey poor, under the direct encouragement and personal supervision of the Slade Professor.

The Guild of St. George took definite shape, and the friendship of some of its chief adherents was a great encouragement and stimulus to Ruskin.   Of these must specially be named the mother of a favourite pupil, Mrs. Talbot of Tyn-y-Ffynon, Barmouth, who in December of 1874 offered him a piece of the cliff overlooking the moor with twelve or thirteen cottages upon it by way of giving the St. George's Guild a start in practical work.   The touching letters that passed between Ruskin and the donor are preserved in Miss Atkinson's pamphlet, *Ruskin's Social Experiment at Barmouth*.   Amongst other things he projected a library of standard literature for the Guild and his co-workers. He set some of his undergraduate friends to the translation of the *Economist* of Xenophon, and lent Brantwood to them for their working, they in return translating Xenophon in the morning, and digging his boat harbour for him in the afternoon.

He came north by way of Derbyshire and joined them in their task in the summer of 1875 ; and there, at the age of fifty-six, he began seriously to consider how much time was likely to be left to him to complete the designs for which he had been collecting material until he was past fifty.

The next year, 1876, now Slade Professor for the third period of three years, he had but a glimpse of Brantwood; but he saw it at the right time, when the larches had not yet lost their tenderest green, when the lambs were white in the near fields, and the voice of the cuckoo was heard in the land. Such time as he spent there was probably occupied with arrangements for setting on foot the St. George's Museum near Sheffield. He passed most of the autumn and winter abroad ; it was not till the middle of the next July, 1877, that he found himself once more within pleasant sight of the Thwaite. He came back from the study of the Dragon of Car- paccio to battle with the steam dragon of our day. The projected extension of the railway from Windermere to Ambleside roused him to noble wrath, as all may see who read his preface to Robert Somervell's protest against the extension of railways in the Lake district, reprinted in *On the Old Road.* But that he had time to think of the mysteries of the decked earth and of the movements of streams and flowing of lava, is apparent from the lecture he delivered the same autumn in Kendal on "Yewdale and its Streamlets."

Very pleasant it is to think of him that July, walking along among the fern by the side of the Yewdale stream to its curve in the meadow, noting the quiet pause of its brown eddy under the root of the oak tree, and bringing all his stream-tracking of years into focus with the question, how came a pool to be there, what was the process or the power that made it?

And not less pleasant to watch him gazing at the squirrel in the tree above, "whilst the little dark-eyed miracle of the forest glanced from branch to branch, more like a sunbeam than a living creature," which inspired him to give his Kendal audience one of the most exquisite descriptions of squirrel life and movement that our English literature contains.

In the May of this year, 1877, he had written from Venice that "after such indexed

summary of his *Fors Clavigera* as he might
be able to give in the seventh volume, he
should set aside the political work he had
intended by it and enter into his own rest,"
that rest really being new service in way of
"bye-law books of botany and geology for
St. George's schools, together with so much
law of art as he might explain or exhibit
under the foul condition of the age."

To this end—the completion of the seventh
volume of *Fors*—he devoted much of his time
at Brantwood in the autumn, and it is clear
that what with his Oxford lectures on hand, his
lectures in the North, his *Fors*, and sorrow of
heart at the apparent falling away of certain
whom he had counted on as friends to his
views and his cause, the strain was too great.

"Amid hope and sorrow, amid fear and
wrath, believe every day that has dawned
on thee to be the last," was all he could send
a friend by way of Christmas message to his
Aberdeen Bible class.

The cloud was falling upon him.   He
struggled hopefully against the over-fatigue
of brain and heart all that January and February of 1878.   But he had scarcely finished
his last *Fors* and the preface to the catalogue
of his *Turners* at the Fine Art Gallery in

New Bond Street, when inflammation of the brain supervened, and the people who crowded the Fine Art Gallery in the first week of March saw the announcement of his illness and read the daily bulletin.

I have in this month of July, 1900, been going round the same gallery to see the same pictures with the same catalogue in hand, and the sorrowful anxiety for the Master's health which then possessed one has come back with painful memory.

There in the preface stands that touching passage of the indefatigable worker : " Morning breaks as I write, along those Coniston fells, and the level mists motionless and grey, beneath the rose of the moorland, veil the lower woods and the sleeping village, and the long lawns of the lake shore," with its bitter cry, " Oh that some one had told me in my youth, when all my heart seemed to be set on these colours and clouds that appear for a little while and then vanish away, how little my love of them would serve me when the silence of lawns and wood in the dew of the morning should be completed and all my thoughts should be of those whom by neither I was to meet more." It has different significance for one now.

One read that passage then, and felt it contained the reason of the breakdown, and its blank despair of help made one's heart ache. One reads it again to-day and one feels that by some other lake and other meadows more purely fair and full of peace than the meadows of Home-ground and Brant-wood—beneath heavens more filled with glory than any that bend above the Coniston fells, he surely walks to-day unpained of soul, and has met, not ever to be parted with, all he loved.

Thanks to the quiet of Brantwood and the tender nursing of friends, he rallied, and after change of air at Malham was back again at his lakeland home working away at his botany, writing up the work of his friend Burne Jones, and embroiling himself in a lawsuit by his hasty dispatch of Mr. Whistler's work with criticism of contempt in *Fors*. What during the weeks of invalidism of this year, the kind angels of the Thwaite did to cheer and help back to strength, may be read in the letter of thanks Ruskin writes under date Nov. 26 : " I have," says he, " entirely resigned all hope of ever thank-ing you rightly for bread, sweet odours, roses and hearts, and must just allow myself to be fed, scented, rose-garlanded as if I were a poor little pet dog or pet pig. But my cold is better, and I am getting on with this botany."

Early in 1879, with the weight of sixty years upon his shoulders, and the weakness of his late illness still hanging about him, he resigned the Slade Professorship, and henceforth the English lakes were to be his home, and the centre of such activity as remained to him. He was busy in the spring of this year in getting his Oxford minerals to Brantwood. At the suggestion of a neighbour clergyman, who was the secretary of a famous Clerical Society, he undertook to help the clergy of the district, or such as cared to be helped, to what he conceived to be a right understanding of the Lord's prayer. It was characteristic of him that he listened to all criticisms that were passed upon his trenchant and eloquent exposition, and answered them with affectionate patience and tender regard for all who differed from him.

It was a matter of regret to many of his friends that he did not shew the same tolerant temper in speaking and writing of some of the bishops, notably the Bishop of Manchester, which he had shewed the country clergy of the Archdeaconry of Westmoreland, but it was patent to all that neither Ruskin nor Bishop Fraser really understood the viewpoints of the other on the question of commercial expediency and morality, and neither was able to convince the other. It almost seemed as if in his vehement hatred of usury the Master had bishops on the brain.

In 1880, from April to August, he was working away at Brantwood at his crystals and his *Fors*, on a series of papers on 'Fiction, Fair and Foul,' and an essay on Scott. He had so much recovered health that he could in one of his chatty letters tell Miss Susie Beever on June 27th how he had that morning written in his diary, " On the whole I never felt better in my life ; mouth, eyes, head, feet, fingers, all fairly in trim ; older than they were, yes, but if the head and heart grow wiser they won't want feet or fingers some day."

Thence away he went to the Continent for the writing of his *Bible of Amiens*, and did not return to Brantwood till the first of December. In January, 1881, we hear of him giving all the Coniston village children a New Year's treat. We see him looking sharply after his gardeners in the conservatory

to prevent them rooting out his favourite
pinks and strawberries to make way for 'nasty
gloxinias and glaring fuchsias.' We see him
still an early riser, bending in the morning
over the MSS. of the *Bible of Amiens*, and
in July can watch him at Seascale sketching
on the shore. But in 1882 he leaves Brantwood to stay at Herne Hill—year memorable
to him, for that though two of his friends,
Rossetti and Dr. John Brown, passed away,
he gained two friends, the writer of the *Story
of Ida*—the collector and illustrator of the
Roadside Songs of Tuscany—and Miss Kate
Greenaway.

He went abroad this year with his biographer, W. G. Collingwood, but glorious as
the view of Mont Blanc was to him in its
power 'to give him back what loves and
memories were most precious to him,' one
seems to see that the very sight of the fresh
snowfall reminds him of his own Westmoreland hills in winter, and makes him wish to
be back at Brantwood and the Thwaite.
Sunny as the waves of the Gulf of Genoa
were, 'breaking like blue clouds under groves
of olive and palm,' they do but take his mind
to England, and make him wish that they
were the waves of Coniston instead.

The next year, 1883, Brantwood saw much of him.   He had fits of despondency, but on the whole he was much better in general health.   People saw him on the moor, and shepherds met him up the Old Man.   The Slade Professor, the present Sir William B. Richmond, true son of his father that he was, stood aside and made it possible for Ruskin to come back to the Oxford Chair.   If Oxford enjoyed lectures on the Art of England, Coniston was favoured with a lecture on Sir H. Edwards, and the Coniston school children had the delight of seeing a great star globe constructed in their playground, within which the future astronomer of the village might sit and see the constellations rise and wane.

How he loved those village children!   It mattered not if it were Agnes of the Moor or Bessie of 'aboon beck,' he took them all into his heart.   "Here in Coniston," he wrote in *Fors* of that September, "it is almost impossible to meet a child whom it is not a real sorrow again to lose sight of."   It was well for him that he found amongst them at school or play so many friends ; he needed all the sunshine of heart that could be given, for with the last day of the year the windows of the Thwaite were darkened, and one of his

D

truest friends, Mary Beever, breathed her last. That year, 1883, which ended so sadly for him, had yet brought him quiet joy. He saw the practical realisation in a simple way of some of his dreams of happy work and handicraft for the homes of the people. Thanks chiefly to the indefatigable enthusiasm of a true disciple who afterwards did for Cumberland what she did for Westmoreland, the spinning wheels were set agoing again in Langdale, whilst, in the same year, largely owing to the master's teaching and his known desires, an industrial Art experiment in metal and wood work was begun at Keswick, which has since flourished beyond expectation. He heard of these endeavours, and was cheered by them.

In 1884 he took up his parable, and, under the title of the "Storm Cloud," delivered a lecture which, while it dealt with aerial pheno-mena, really dealt with spiritual ones. He was back at Brantwood in March, revising his chapter in *Fors* called 'Retrospect,' in which he propounds his theory of village-child education. Folk who visit the Crosthwaite Boys' School garden and see the little gardeners therein at work may thank Ruskin for having therein written, as a rule with no exception, " Every parish school to have garden, playground, and cultivable land round it or belonging to it."

But most of his time was spent on the preparation of the course of lectures he intended to give in the October term at Oxford on " The Pleasures of England." Between whiles he worked at St. George's Museum, and edited Miss Alexander's *Roadside Songs of Tuscany*, and wrote the last number of *Fors*. But the incessant labour was causing excitement of brain which, though it did not culminate in actual illness, at least unfitted him for the strain of public lectures, and many were glad that he cancelled the last three militant lectures at Oxford, and substituted readings from his earlier works instead.

He came back to Westmoreland in the middle of December to return no more to the city of his one-time love and hope, the city of his soul's disappointment. The vote to allow vivisection by endowing a chair of physiological research fairly broke his heart. He resigned his Professorship, and, to her loss and blame, Oxford ungratefully accepted the resignation.

Mis-statements were made at the time in the press as to his reasons for giving up the

Slade Chair and retiring from the university ;
Ruskin determined that the truth should be
known, and wrote to the *Pall Mall Gazette*
in April of 1885, as follows : "Whatever may
be my failure in energy or ability, the best I
could do was wholly at the service of Oxford.
I meant to die in harness there, and my
resignation was placed in the Vice-Chancellor's
hands on the Monday following the vote
endorsing Vivisection in the university, solely
in consequence of that vote, with distinct
statement to the Vice-Chancellor, intended to
be read in Convocation, of its being so."

1885-6 were years of illness and the cloud.
His wish for work was great as ever, but
his powers to endure brain fatigue very
limited.   As he regained strength he worked
at *Praeterita* and *Dilecta*, and seemed to
be able to shake off the sad present in
memories of the past.   The hills were a
comfort to him, the flowers of his garden
and moor were a joy, Coniston Old Man,
with its half-mile of rainbow upon its breast,
Yewdale Crag, with its constant question,
'How came I to be here?' the lake brought
him something of its deep calm, and the
sunset showered glory on him at eventide.

Always too he had the happiness of know-

ing that at the Thwaite was still one who
honoured him, and cared for all his work.
In a letter, date 22nd May, 1886, he wrote,
"I've been out all the morning and am so
sleepy, but I've written a nice bit of *Praeterita*
before I went out trying to describe the Rhone
at Geneva. I think Susie will like it, if
nobody else." Tender little notes with May-
day gift of agate, sketches sent on loan, keep
up the constant exchange of affection that
passed between the Garden and the Thwaite
in these sad months of illness.

In the late autumn of 1886 he arranged and
wrote the preface for Francesca Alexander's
book, *Christ's Folk in the Apennines*, and interested himself in Mrs. Firth's translation of
Ulric the Farm-Servant. He was scarce
recovered from the second severe illness in
1886 when the shock of hearing of the death of
his much-beloved secretary, young Laurence
Hilliard, seems to have induced another attack,
and his condition was considered critical by his
friends. But he slowly recovered, and in June
was able to shew not only that he was in his
own most sober and serious mind by writing a
trenchant letter to the *Pall Mall Gazette* on
the functions of the press in general and of the
Pall Mall in particular, but in the postscript he

allowed his readers sight of his weariness, and his deep pain that men should mistake the increasing earnestness of his appeals to Britain for right doing as the sign of a disordered brain. The letter may be quoted in its entirety :

The Function of the Pall Mall Gazette.

"SIR,—Permit me, in anxious courtesy, to advise you that the function of the *Pall Mall Gazette* is neither to teach theology nor criticise art.

"You have taken an honest and powerful position in modern politics and ethics : you have nothing whatever to do with traditions of eternal punishment ; but only to bring, so far as you may, immediate malefactors to immediate punishment.

" It is quite immaterial to the great interests of the British nation whether a popular music master be knighted, or left to his simple dignity of troubadour, but it is of infinite importance that the already belted knights of England should speak truth and do justice ; and that the ancient lords of England should hold their power in England, and of Ireland in Ireland, and of Scotland in Scotland, and not gamble and race their estates away, nor live in London club-houses at the cost of their poor tenants.

"These things you have to teach, Sir, and to plead for ; and permit me further to tell you as your constant, but often grieved reader, that as you make your columns in part useless with irrelevant religious debate and art gossip, so you make them too often horrible with records of crime which should be given only in the *Police News*.

"Use your now splendidly organized body of correspondents to find out what is being done by good and wise men under the advancing conditions of our civilization—expose, once for all, the fallacies of dishonest or ignorant politicians, and name them no more. (How much type have you spent, do you suppose, in printing the names of members of the present scratch Parliament who know no more of policy than their parish beadle.)

"Press home whatever wise and gentle and practical truth you find spoken, whether in Parliament or out of it, by men who are seeking for truth and for peace.

"And believe me always your faithful and grateful servant,

"JOHN RUSKIN.

"BRANTWOOD, June 6th (1886).

"I have not written this letter with my usual care, for I am at present tired and sad; but you will enough gather my meaning in it. And may I pray of your kindness, in any notice you grant the continuation of *Praeterita*, to contradict the partly idle, partly malicious rumours which I find have got into other journals respecting my state of health this spring. Whenever I write a word that my friends don't like, they say I am crazy, and never consider what a cruel and wicked form of libel they thus provoke against the work of an old age in all its convictions antagonistic to the changes of the times, and in all its comfort oppressed by them."

This letter is the letter of a man in deadly earnest, but it is the letter of a man sore at the heart. That vexation of heart prevented recovery, and in August he posted with his ever-watchful guardian cousin, Mrs. Severn, to Folkestone for complete change of air and scene. He gained strength, and was able to write, the preface and notes to Mr. E. T. Cook's hand-

book to the National Gallery. I have heard
from one who saw him at Folkestone how the
old longing for his northern home came upon
him, and how with returning strength he
wearied again for the Coniston hills.

The spring of the next year, 1888, was spent
at Sandgate. The strain of writing seemed
more than he could bear, and, without the
writing to occupy him, there was restlessness
that made it seem advisable to try what another,
and that his last, tour to the Continent would
do, to keep him interested and yet give him
rest from actual writing, with such change of
occupation from writing as sketching might be.
But neither the air of Abbeville nor the breezes
of the Jura, nor the sight of Mont Blanc, nor
the calm and sun of the Venetian lagoon could
avail ; and when he returned to Brantwood in
the last week of 1888, he came back depressed
of heart and enfeebled of frame, and none could
have believed other than that he came back to
die.

Such, however, was the restorative charm of
quiet Brantwood, and the watchful care of those
about him, that he rallied in 1889. We hear of
him in June at his favourite little bit of the
Cumberland dunes, Seascale, with its dwarf
roses and its purple geraniums full in flower on

the sand-hills ; and its peep of those hills in the
Wastwater direction, as blue as ever the hills
were blue which his old nurse sang of, as they
crossed the bridge of Tweed.   He still hoped
to finish the third volume of *Praeterita*, and to
bring down the recollections of his life to 1875.
As a matter of fact, he did finish, though with
difficulty, out of the intended nine parts, the one
planned for the conclusion of the volume.

We who read that Part IV., entitled
'Joanna's Care,' can have little idea of the
pathetic pain it cost him, though we may guess
how glad the workman, as he worked at this,
his last task, surely was to leave behind a
monument of such affection and regard for her
who had been the nearest companion of his
home and happiness and heart-break, for her who
was to be his constant helpmeet still until the
end.

Ruskin returned from Seascale to the Brantwood of his love that he never again should
leave till tender hands should bear him to his
grave.   The days of his age were threescore
years and ten, and none who saw him in that
year of 1889 would have thought it likely that
he would be numbered amongst those who
'are so strong that they come to fourscore
years.'

But for him it was decreed that ten long
years of silence and patience should be fulfilled
before he should pass to the land where the
spirits of men who have laboured, as he
laboured, for truth and righteousness, are
strong with the strength of the Lord.

There is no need to tell of that time. There
were alternations of deep melancholy and
hopeful peace. There was one great sorrow,
the death of Miss Susie Beever in 1893. The
storm-cloud of sorrow and pain and loss finally
rolled away, and his heart, as happy as a child
that goes unto its father, had rest.

Nor is there a need to speak of the days
and ways of Brantwood between 1872 and
1889. For the constant courtesies of the host,
and the genial welcomings to all true friends,
are chronicled for us delightfully by Mrs.
Ritchie, Miss Wakefield, and Mr. Collingwood.

They who have ever been privileged to be
so welcomed will bear testimony to the way in
which the Master of the House fed soul as he
cared for body of all he entertained. And
since the gift without the giver is bare, he
gave himself, his 'heart affluence in discursive
talk,' his time, so precious to such a worker,
and all his enthusiasm, without stint and without reserve to his guests.

But for myself, who walked with and talked with some of the older folk and shepherds in those earlier years of Ruskin's residence in Brantwood, it is pleasantest to remember that "t'girt Perfessor," as they called him, "for aw he was high larnt," had won their hearts by his courtesy to themselves, and his tender kindness to their children, and was welcomed at all doors.

CHAPTER III.

REMINISCENCES OF RUSKIN AMONG THE PEASANTRY OF CONISTON.

I WAS standing to-day, 7th February, 1900, at the grave of one of the last prophets of our generation, and thinking how true was his saying, that the pulpit which could send its message furthest was the grave.

To-morrow is John Ruskin's birthday. If he had been spared to us a few weeks, he would to-morrow have entered on his 82nd year. One could not wish him back again, except that he might hear the voices of praise and thankfulness for his long battle for the Truth and Right, which have gone up to Heaven ceaselessly from all corners of the land, since "God's finger touched him and he slept."

His grave is not yet a fortnight old. Some of the wreaths that covered his coffin still lie

upon the ground—veiled to-day as it is by the
pure garniture of snow; others hang touched
into bronze by the hand of the bitter cold upon
the three crosses, close by, that mark the resting-place of his friends, the "Ladies of the
Thwaite."

How deeply and affectionately his words are
held in remembrance—how truly he being dead
yet speaketh, could never have been known,
had he lived to be a hundred, as has come to
be realised within the compass of these few
short days.

The very foot-marks in the heavy snowfall
are eloquent. All who have entered the churchyard since the snow came have bent their steps
one way to the quiet north-east corner of the
burial-ground, where the deodars and pines
seem to keep of right a guardian watch above
the sleep of the man in Europe who best understood the beauty of their kind and wrote
glowingly of their nature and their form and
service.

But if he were with us once again to behold
the fairness of this winter valley as I see it
to-day, I am sure he would ask us to turn from
the spot where he rests. He would point to
the unsightly sheds and roof-trees over there,
of coldly-gleaming slate, that entirely mar the

beauty of the hillside towards the west. He
would bid us come away with him up Yewdale
to the Tilberthwaite gorge—a wondrous fissure
in the flanks of Wetherlam. He would delight
to shew us, as we passed backward and forward
over the torrent by the bridges he thoughtfully
planned, how glorious was the jewelry with
which the frost giant decked the torrent! The
joy of his first sight of icicles in Glenfarg
haunted him all his life.

He has lived for years past almost within
sight of a Scandinavian scholar at Torver, and
been in constant communication with Mr.
Collingwood, a lover of the Vikings, so that
perhaps he would fall to talking of the time
when children of the dale would first hear tale
of trolls and frost giants, would tell us of the
days when under the Viking 'Thorstein of the
Mere' the king's town rose beside the waters of
the lake and won its name of Thurston-Water.

Thence would he bid us retrace our steps by
the Yewdale Farm, with its giant chessman
wrought in the living yew-tree hedge, and
pausing he would ask us to remember how
often that Yewdale Crag, lifting solid and sheer
from the vale, had borne him back in mind to
the Mount of God, and made him think of the
commandments of law and obedience he strove

to fill with spirit, and teach to a disobedient and impatient time.

Thence passing over the stream whereby, in spring, the *noli-me-tangere* balsam grows, he would assuredly lead us upward to Tarn House and bid us realise the beauty of the hills from Walney Scar and Coniston Old Man by Wetherlam, Grey Friars, Crinkle Crags and Bowfell to the Pikes and far Scafell, all clad to-day in ermine washed with gold, or pointing southward down beyond the umber woods and the white meadow-land and grey-black hedge-rows, shew us how fair a mirror for the gleaming cloud was tranquil Coniston Lake from end to end.

But as we gaze from the Farm House upland this afternoon over the sunny winter scene, our eyes seem constantly to search along the eastern shore for that white gleaming spot of light in the darkened wood where never more can come to those who looked for his welcome the light of hope and tender greeting where for us, at anyrate, with gloom that even this bright after-noon sun cannot drive away, the shadow of death has been laid, and the sense of absence and of loss to the nation deepens with every dawn.

And yet, and yet, how fair is the scene, how glowingly the red fern and the beechen hedges stand against the snow, how full of quiet colour of puce and brown the copses along the Brantwood slopes sweep from the lake mirror of golden grey up to those bossy Hawkshead fells, where in old boyhood days Wordsworth visited his woodcock springes and went away ashamed!

How gloriously against the already purpling birch the larches seem to stand like feathered bronze, and gleam as if they felt the springtide sure was nigh.

The shadows on the far-off fells are deepest blue, the tracks of rabbits that have written their capital 'Ys' upon the snow are filled with cobalt on the bank at my side, and whitely against an apple green north stand up the towers of the circling hills, made whiter by the deep green junipers and the bronze-red of the bracken foreground.

But it is at the Coniston Old Man and Wetherlam one gazes longest. These, grey against the yellowing evening sky, mount up into heaven, and seem so to grow against the gathering glory that one wonders if those eyes that more than other eyes have looked with love upon them would not now confess that even our Lake Country hills are not "always too low to be perfectly sublime"; that indeed under some atmospheric conditions the same

RUSKIN'S WAY-SIDE REST NEAR BRANTWOOD.

From Photo. by H. Bell.

feeling in kind, though perhaps not in degree, may be given to the heart that seeks for the glory of God upon the shoulders of Wetherlam, as is showered upon it on the Wengern Alp or under the hills of Engelberg.

To-day the waves of the white mountain are lifted to heaven in a stillness of perpetual peace, the croak of a far-off raven, a cock-crow at a distant farm, or the bleating of a cluster of sheep about their hay racks in the vale are all the sounds that break the silence.

But across the stillness I hear the voice I heard of old, saying "that the most helpful and sacred work for humanity that can now be done is to teach people the art of joy in humble life, the life full of sensitiveness to all elements of costless and kind pleasure, and therefore chiefly to the loveliness of the natural world." I hear the Teacher saying "the men who love nature most will always be found to have most capability for faith in God," that "if you would cultivate admiration, you must be among beautiful things and looking at them," and I wonder as I stand here gazing upon a scene of beauty in which "the whole heart of nature seems thirsting to give and still to give," why it is that the prophets of our time have been so silent on this matter; why it is that we have

E

left that one grave in the valley at our feet, to
preach to the simple people of our land the
everlasting gospel of peace and pleasure, of
strength and purity, that come of communion
with the spirit of God, and joy in the work of
His hands.

Even as I gaze far down to that quiet
pulpit by the church in the grey 'Town of
the King' by the mere, and think of him
who is now beholding another King in His
beauty in the land that is very far off, I seem
to feel the challenge of his brave heart that,
like the heart of Nature he wrote of, was
"ever thirsting to give and still to give,"
to take up his gospel message and to cry
aloud to the people that they are losing
strength and health to their nation's life by
refusing the mediatorial ministry of these hills
and vales, whose higher mission is "to fill
the thirst of the human heart for the beauty
of God's work, and to startle its lethargy
with the deep and pure agitation of astonishment." To go to the schoolmasters of the
land and bid them understand that 'true love
of Nature' is precisely the most healthy
element which distinctively belongs to us,
and that out of it, cultivated no longer in
levity or ignorance, but in earnestness and

as a duty, "may arise new revelations of the
nature of man's life, and of the true relations
between him and his Maker."

Yes, the grave beside the deodars and
pines there in the valley may be closed, but
the voice that told us that the love of Nature
wherever it has existed has been 'a faithful
and a sacred element of feeling,' is a voice
of comfort for the humblest poor to-day.

As I thought on these things a shepherd
came from the fell ; tenderly and patiently he
was taking the little mountain sheep, that
looked almost black against the snow, down
to the valley. " Yes, poor things," he said,
"they're hungered to death amoast and
they're tie'd to be. They hev been pecklin'
about amang t' heather for a day or two, but
snaw pinches them terbly for pasture. Heyjak!
Heyjak! get away hint! Down with the'!"
and the collie at his word sat like a stone,
while the shy little mountaineers passed
slowly and with diffidence through the fell
gate.

" Did you know Mr. Ruskin?" I said.

" What, th' Professor? ay, ay, and ivery
shepherd for miles round kenned him an aw.
He hedn't a bit o' pride hedn't t' Professor,
and he was partickler fond of a crack about

dogs and sheep. I member yan time, he
meede up a beuk aboot sheepfoelds, and a
gentleman fra Lunnon, as hed stayed wi' us
in t' summer time, sent yan doon til us, but
be hanged to it, theer was nowt aboot our
traade in it from first leaf to last. By gock,
what a gay good laugh Professor hed, and
how he clapped his hands togedder when
my missis telt him."

"But what struck you most about the
Professor?"

"Well, well, that he hedn't a bit o' pride
aboot him. Wad crack on same as if he
was owder you or me. He a girt professor,
and me nobbut a fell-shepherd. But he was
most partickler fond of the sheep and dogs
and birds and aw mak of things that hed life.
Kindest hearted man as ivver was to ony-
thing that hed a bit o' life in it was th'
Professor now. But it wasn't only sheep and
dogs he was partial to, he was gaily weel
pleased with flowers and ferns an' aw, and
I 'member he was yance up here latin' mosses
and what not, and he shewed me a bit of
them colourments upon the steans, nay I
can't mind on what he cawed them, but he
was pleased as a child wid yan o' 'em on a
boulder stean, and talked for iver of it."

My shepherd friend had read from time to time 'bits of the Professor's writings out o' the papers,' but he had never read that passage in which the Professor, who now lies waiting for the meek mosses and grey lichens to do their last sweet service for him, and take up their tender watch by his headstone, had spoken of these 'creatures full of pity, laying quiet fingers on the trembling stones to teach them rest,' with traceries of intricate silver, and fringes of amber, lustrous, arborescent, burnished through every fibre into fitful brightness and glossy traverses of silken change.

Nor had the shepherd at Tarn House, with staff in hand, who even as he spoke was playing havoc with a golden lichen-spot, star-like upon the stone beside him, ever heard how the Professor had written of lichens as "Humblest and most honoured of earth-children; strong in loveliness, neither blanched in heat nor pined in frost," nor of how Ruskin had once described them thus: "To them slow-fingered, constant-hearted, is entrusted the wearing of the dark eternal tapestries of the hills, to them slow-pencilled, iris-dyed, the tender framing of their endless imagery."

"Well, well, did he say all this aboot 'em poor things? 'Well, to be seuer!' I knaw they

mak a terble deal of goldy stuff an' especially
at sunset time on Yewdale Crag, and my lad
often telt they was gay-good map-makers and
aw, but t' Professor seed a deal mair than moast
fwoks, and you nivver met him widout a laal
bit o moss, or a stean, or a flower i' his hand.

"He was fond of iverything in t'daale, and
partickler fond o' barns. School childer wad
wait for him at lonning-end just on chance
of a word or a pat o' t' head fra t' Professor.
Eh, dear! I mind how he wad be off at times
to Dame school on Hawkshead Brow just
for plessur of seeing th' barns; how the lads
and lasses would get him to sit on their laal
bit sled-cart, and trail him up th' hill, and he
wad hev' the girls tie up their hair wi' bright
ribands, and wad say they sud hev' warm
bright cloaks in winter time, and be proud of
their dress, but hev' it good sensible mak' for
wear and tear, saame as in old time, when
fwoks wove by hand. Then he would hev'
a luk in at joiner's shop, or at builder's, or
at smithy, and if he chanced upon a fisher-
man or a boatman on t' lake, when he was
in his 'Jumping Jenny,' as he cawed his oan
boat, nowt wud sarve but he must hev' a
crack wid him. Nivver seed a man so plaain
in his waays wi' fwok.

"I 'member yance of a time when he and yan they cawd Bell hed a crack aboot politics and sec-like, and William clapped Perfessor on t' shoulder—he was vara friendly wid him ye kna—and he said, 'Well, to my waays o' thinking, for aw your conservative talk and writings and what not, you are as radical as t' best on us.' And Perfessor leuked oop wid a smile and smacked his hand intil William's, and he said, 'Well, well, you're not so far wrong efter aw.' But he was terble humble-minded, heddn't a bit o' pride aboot him, I telt ye; he tret poor and rich alike, it wadn't a mattered a pin whedder it was a lord or a sarvin' man, if he could hev' deun owt for ever he wad a deun it. Theer was a nebbur, a woman body, I mind, as sent him a basket o' pears, and Perfessor was pleased as owt, and why, nowt wad sarve but he mud write a letter to her saame as if she was the Queen, and ask permission to coom doon along o' Mrs. Severn theer and see her gardin and give her his best thanks. I've seen letter scoors o' times. He hedn't a lock o' friends aboot him, and as for barns, he was fairly barn-mad. I remember when Wilkinson's barn got snecked in t' leg, poor thing, in t' scythe in the lang grass, and

died, the Perfessor was craazed omoast wi'
grief, and wad gang and sit wi' fwok at the
Moor for lang eneuf."

As the shepherd spoke I remembered that
passage in the last volume of *Fors* where, after
describing one of his visits to the house, and
the joy of the younger brother at the return
home of the sister, Jane Anne, he continues,
" But the dearest child of the cottage was
not there.   Last spring they had a little
boy between these two, full of intelligent life,
and pearl of chief price to them.   He went
down into the field by the brookside (Beck
Leven) one bright morning when his elder
brother was mowing.   The child came up
behind without speaking and the back sweep
of the scythe caught the leg and divided a
vein.   His brother carried him up to the
house ; and what swift binding could do was
done—the doctor three miles away coming
as soon as might be, arranged all for the
best, and the child lay pale and quiet till the
evening, speaking sometimes a little to his
father and mother.   But at six in the evening
he began to sing—sang on clearer and clearer
all through the night, so clear at last you
might have heard him, his mother said, 'far
out on the moor there.'   Sang on till the

full light of morning and so passed away."
" Did he sing with words ? " I asked. " Oh
yes, just the bits of hymns he had learnt
at Sunday School."

Ah, thought I, how little the shepherd
realised that the love of child-life was a passion
with the Master. Other correspondents might
have to wait for his answers to their enquiries,
but a child, never. It was a fortunate thing
for Ruskin—though perhaps it was not always
so well for the children, for he spoiled them
at times—that the village bairns were fair to
see. " Here in Coniston," he once wrote, " it
is almost impossible to meet a child whom it
is not a real sorrow again to lose sight of."
The shepherd did not know how that homeli-
ness and unaffected simplicity of address which
made Ruskin so approachable to child or man
was the work of a long life's discipline. The
shyest of men, he had made himself the servant
of all, and judged by his own standard his
greatness had lain just there.

" Every great man," he once said, " is always
being helped by everybody, for his gift is to
get good out of all things and all persons."

Nor did my shepherd friend know how
deeply the Professor had entered into the innate
nobility of the dalesman life. How he had

once put it on record that at his gate were
living persons of yeoman stock whose word
was their bond, and who for manner and
nobility of life might have been knights at
Agincourt.

It was good to have had a 'crack' with the
shepherd; it was not only that he knew how
the Professor had been welcome at every fellside farm and cottage door in the days when
he 'was stirrin' aboot, ye kna,' but it made one
see how truly Ruskin had tried to carry out in
his daily life among the Coniston people his
teaching of sympathy with labour and lowly life
in fair surroundings, and how he had in his
goings in and out amongst the people, shewn or
striven to shew that the dalesman's life of
domestic affection and domestic peace, if it
were full of 'sensitiveness to all elements of
costless and kind pleasure and, therefore, here,—
among the mountains and by the mere,—chiefly
to the loveliness of the natural world,' was a life
that ought to satisfy and could satisfy the souls
of men.

I went back in mind to the day of the burial
in the 'God's acre' at our feet. I realised how
entirely in harmony it must have been with this
lover of the simple dalesman life, that though
the great ones of the earth were not present,

the shepherds and cottagers and farming folk
had come from far away to see 'th' last of t'
awld Professor,' whom they honoured, because
he honoured them.   From far away?   Yes
from far-off Manchester one mourner had come,
a student of the Master's works, and he a
butcher boy.

"It's likely gitten late," said the shepherd,
"sun 'll be behint Wetherlam in ten minutes,
I'm thinking.   Sheep wants suppering up, and
I'se not so sewer but what I cud do wit a bit of
poddish mysel.'"

Down to the deep white glistening vale he
went, and I clomb up one of the Tarn House
knolls to watch the eve of the 81st birthday of
the Professor die beyond the hills.

The low sun made all the level snowfield
seem suddenly a mass of miniature mountains,
each casting its lilac-blue shadow.   The tracks
of the sheep and the shepherd's footmarks
shone as if they were lemon-gold.   As for the
beech hedges by the plantation, and the bracken
above the snow, it gleamed almost as if it were
fresh from a molten furnace.   Then the blue
shadows faded from the snowfield, and while on
the upper fells the glory of the yellow golden
light seemed to grow and grow, the sun had
sunk, leaving a dusky orange light above the

hills, and in a moment the radiance passed from the earth, and Coniston Old Man, and Wetherlam and Grey Friars seemed smitten with the ashy pallor of death.

Yet the sky was still full of light and loveliness. The orange faded into light amber, and the amber climbed upward to a pale green at the zenith. Suddenly all the far-off heights to the east went from gold to rose, and even the Furness Fells and the snowfields of the lower heights blushed visibly.

But the rose-light did not linger long on far-off peak or nearer Furness Fells. The glow seemed to leap into mid air, and the whole east glowed with rosy purple light. I watched till beneath the rose in the eastern sky a blue vapour seemed to mount toward mid-heaven, and mix its lucent blueness with the rosy blush. When I turned my eyes from the east to the west, I found the same wonderful lemon-gold palpitating to the zenith; and just where the green light overhead seemed to hold a kind of balance between the blue east and the golden west, I saw the half-moon hang its silver shield, and one star, and that the star of Love, had lighted the lamp of its glory.

I went down into the vale by the half light of moon and afterglow, and as I walked toward the village the shadows lay delicately pencilled upon the snow, by the branches of the oak and ash, each twig black and clear, the whole intricate tracery defined by moonlight magic's draughtsmanship. When I reached the church-yard, and stood for the last time by the gentle Professor's grave, I felt not a little comforted to think that though his sun had set, the person-ality he had left behind to brighten even as the waxing moon was brightening, could give such light and beauty to the darkened vale as should serve to guide the feet of every wanderer in the night to their far-off home.

Leaving the quiet grave over which the moonlit snow seemed to lay a pall of silver beauty, made more apparent by contrast of the dark shadows of the pine and deodars in the background, I climbed the hill.

The snowfall had so hushed the road that one almost heard 'the beating of one's heart.' An owl tu-whooed from the wood, and gained a far-off answer from the Brantwood groves; all else was silent. The lake glimmered and the flanks of Wetherlam and Coniston Old Man gleamed through the frosty air. On any other night one might have felt the loneliness of the road, but all the way the Professor seemed to be with one.

That grave had veritably yielded up its dead;
and not with long white beard and bended
form, but lithe and alert and full of fun as
of old, when he led us to our labours in the
Hinksey lane, or swore us in, as knights of his
Table Round, in the rooms at Corpus, the dear
and honoured friend and teacher walked and
talked beside one.

The very heavens seemed to sparkle for him
to-night.   He had written that there were
worse things than war, and lo! Orion with his
gleaming blade hung regent of the south.   He
had by a few masterly strokes of his pen
glorified forever the plowman's work afield, and
lo! in the north the starry constellation was set
to plowing the hills of heaven.   He had called
us with appealing music of thought and sound
back from the clamorous cities of dreadful night,
to the quiet cornlands of the country life of
sower and reaper in sweet country air, and lo!
at the zenith gleamed the sickle set with stars!

And so up the silent road and down the
Hawkshead hill I went, in communion with the
spirit of a man whose thought will not pass
from English life till men cease to look with
gladness for the dawn or to gaze with ardour
upon a sunsetting and lift no more their eyes
with wonder to the stars.

CHAPTER IV.

AT THE RUSKIN EXHIBITION, CONISTON.

ON the most glorious day of a glorious July we found ourselves passing down the Derwent Vale, filled with the scent of its hay-swathes and fragrant from the patches of meadow-sweet which the mowers had left in the field corners, on our way to the sea-coast *en route* for Coniston.

The Solway lay blue almost as the Mediterranean, and Criffel shone like grey marble across the flood, while Mona's isle lay humped like some gigantic whale on the westward horizon. We passed Derwent's mouth, with its memories of St. Cuthbert. We passed Harrington, with its tradition of that famous missal of St. Cuthbert washed ashore and so saved to the thanksgiving of the monks who were heartbroken for its loss, and to the gain of our British Museum authorities of to-day. We

went by ancient Bega's home, and thoughts of
the snow miracle on mid-summer day brought a
pleasant sense of cool into the air.   We passed
Ravenglass, and dreamed of the days when
the Roman general, as he stood now on the
western limit of his world, looked out across
the gleaming waterflood, and wondered if other
lands to conquer lay beyond.   We seemed once
more back among Arabian sandhills by the gulf
of Akaba, as we saw the azure-blue water of a
high tide fill the sand-locked harbour of King
Aveling's town, sparkle up the Vale of Esk,
and lose itself among the woods of Muncaster.
Drigg and its memory of the Druid oak groves
of old time was left behind; Whitbeck was
glanced at, nestling under that mighty hill of
Black Combe that laid such weight upon the
poet Faber's mind—Black Combe that from
some mysterious power of impressing men of
old had its mountain skirts one time broidered
with the stone circles of the sun worshippers.
We went by the opening to Whicham Vale,
beloved of the Sir Lancelot of Faber's poem—
by Millom and its gibbet field, where the Lords
of Millom did dread judgment of yore.   So,
across the sands and samphire fields at the
mouth of Duddon Vale, white with the wings
of the gull, loud with the bleating of sheep, we

sped.   We saw the Broughton village and its church and yews nestle under the sloping fell in the near distance, while far away grey and beautiful the Coniston Old Man leaned against a deep blue sun-filled heaven.   From Foxfield Junction we turned our backs upon the sea and samphire flats and passed into the bosom of the hills.   Patches of hay—fields freshly gathered shone out like emerald from among the oaken copses, and pleasant cottages, with the nasturtium already bright in flower upon their milk-white walls, peeped at us as we went along.

Two or three unpretentious stations that seemed almost as if they were part of the fell-side woodland were stopped at.   Then some one at my side said, "That is Brantwood!" There across the shining waterflood and underneath the dark woodland of the Furness Fell shone out—much more magnificently than that humble cottage home which the poet and engraver had known of old, the retreat of the last poet of the English Lakes, the late John Ruskin.

All along by the shore of the Thurston-water was a strip of brightest green, half-screened by a fringe of trees that seemed to grow almost out of the water, so near were they to the marge.   Beyond this long strip of green were the walls and hedges of a single road ; beyond this again steeply, or ' brant,' as the northerners say, rose up the plantation of oak and birch and hazel, that passed upward into larchen groves, and filled all the slope of the eastern side of the valley with darkened shadow.

Whitely at the base of the woodland shone Brantwood and its neighbouring Lodge. The eyes, caught up by the rosy light upon the heather on the higher fells, perceived that above and to the right of Brantwood the great woodland had one time been felled, and in the clearing gleamed green fields and a single cottage farm. This was the Moor, or more exactly Lawson Park, with its old memories of the times of the monks of Furness. For it was they and their servants who first tilled the soil and tended the flocks at the Park Farm on the moor. One could trace from Brantwood the steep path by which the shepherd sought his upland home. How many a time had the Professor, wearied with his long morning's work, climbed that path for happy intercourse and household chat with the simple fellside folk ; how often had he gazed with jealous eye upon that little wood-encircled enclosure which was to him a veritable Naboth's vineyard.

But the train went hurrying on, suddenly

below us on our right, but on this side of the lake stood up the towery-looking chimneys of the quaint old Coniston Hall which had so attracted Ruskin's eyes, when he was an under-graduate tourist, that he must needs sketch it, to illustrate his ideas of rightful chimney-building, in his essay on the Poetry of Architecture.

Now we have won Coniston, and leaving the train and passing out of the station we ask ourselves if ever mortal felt as he left a train so suddenly transported into the world of mountain quietude. We are turned out upon the fellside breast, a picturesque farm-cottage is close by ; in front, a magnificent Scotch fir stands darkly against the sunshine on Long Crags. A road runs winding up the Walney scar and Coniston Old Man, and a mountain streamlet murmurs in our ears.

Down into the village we go—village strangely jumbled up with picturesque confusion as far as streets or roadways go, but village strangely wanting in picturesque dwellings.

We cross the Coniston or Mines Beck, to-day clear as crystal ; to our left the street leads us off towards the Coniston Institute and the famous collection of Ruskin drawings, which we

have come so far to see. To the right the
main street leads towards the church and so to
Waterhead.

We cannot go to see the work of the dead
master before we have paid the tribute of
memory by standing for a moment at his grave
side. It is evident that we are but one of
thousands who so have thought and felt, for
the grass has been worn into bareness all the
way from the gravel path across the churchyard ground to the north-east corner, where
'amicably close' there stand the three white
crosses that tell us of the resting of his friends.
There, to the north of these three graves of the
'Ladies of the Thwaite,' lies the simple mound,
a single wreath of flowers upon it, that marks
the spot where the master's body lies. A little
black board upon the wall close by tells us that
the un-named grave is his.

How sadly, for all the sweet July sunshine,
do the deodars whisper round his rest, and
we go forth from the graveyard to the museum
in the Institute with a heavy heart.

What strikes one at once about the collection
of pictures that are now on exhibition there, is
the prodigious amount of work that they are
evidence of, and the next thing is that they are
so skilfully selected and arranged as to be a

kind of guide to the whole life's-work of John
Ruskin.

A little guide-book is put into our hands.
The poppies gracefully imprinted from a wood-
block on the cover tell us that the master has
fallen upon sleep, and opening it we find that
the compiler, Mr. Collingwood—to whose indefatigable industry and love we owe the realising
of the idea of this collection—assures us that
these drawings have been arranged chronologi-
cally, that they are a pictorial biography in
themselves, that they are by no means all that
exist, but that there are many fine examples in
Oxford, London, Sheffield and elsewhere, and
in America, but that here may be seen specimens from all Ruskin's varied phases and
periods.

As one passes on from phase to phase, one's
astonishment grows that Ruskin could ever
have found time to draw with such exceeding
delicacy and detail, and at the same time write
with such marvellous *labor limae*, the mass of
work he left behind him.   The next thing that
one marvels at is, how with so little actual
colour work he was such a colourist ; witness
his drawing of the rock opal and the sketch
from above Thun or of the Towers of Fribourg.
But before going round the collection of this

master draughtsman's work, this legacy to
shame us into industry, let us come close to
the man.

He too was once a helpless infant with only
the thoughts of a little child. But he had
parents who believed that God could still
shrine himself in mortal flesh, take the child's
heart and make it a fit temple for His spirit.
Here is the little christening robe that careful
hands embroidered, the tiny bell-like cap, the
little shirt which was worn that day in 1819,
when he was given unto God and consecrated
to the service 'of Christ unto his life's end' at
the church font. And he too was once only
pleased as babes are pleased with toys; here are
the silver bells and the coral that he shook
delightedly as he lay in his cradle. As I gaze
upon them I cannot but doubt that even then
the silver bells brought him thoughts he could
not utter, trained his ear to that delicate perception of sweet sound that made him such a
master of harmonious language as he wrote his
prose poems—that even then, the baby's eye
was trained to love of colours, and to wonder
at form, by the shining coral in his hand.

Not far from the little christening cap lies
a miniature, a good copy of the picture—in
the Brantwood dining-room—of his mother.

It is worth careful study. The brightness and keenness and vivacity of the face, the grey blue eyes, are tokens to us of how much even in outward appearance he owed to that mother. It may be fancy, but one seems to see behind the face all that puritan power which, though it doubtless helped, as the cold mutton on Sunday helped, to prevent John Ruskin becoming an evangelical bishop, did yet contrive to ground him in such knowledge of the psalms and Bible as remained with him a heritage of thought and diction throughout life.

Here are the writer's inkstand and pen, the weapons of our 19th century gladiator; there his seal; no grey white, half-transparent chalcedony was ever put to nobler use. For every seal the Master made therewith told those who broke the sealing that a time would come when no work could be done, that 'To-day, to-day, to-day,' was the appointed time, and that men must work while they have the light, and serve to-morrow by using well 'to-day.'

Close by lies the open colour-box and brushes and pencil. As one looks at it, one feels much as one felt when looking a few weeks ago at the withered skeletons of colour in the rude case which Turner used; that with

so little, so insignificant a bit of furniture the
workman should be able to work such charm;
this it is that astonishes one. But for me
who often saw the chain upon his neck and
often noted the tenderness with which he
would place his watch before him on the
desk at the beginning of his Oxford lectures,
my interest seemed centred in the watch that
needs no longer to keep pace with sun or
star. Then there is the little lens he used
to examine the wonders of the lichen growth
upon the walls or marvel of mineral structure
or texture of fine painting, when he would
peer further than ordinary human eye may
see. Near it rests the hammer he swung to
such purpose in his geological rambles. But
most touching, and seeming to bring the
student and philosopher back into such human
relationship with the peasant life and the
wild-wood life around him, lie the gloves and
the bill-hook he so often used in the ' Brant
Wood ' by the shore of Coniston.

It was a privilege to have in one's hand
the carefully written catalogue which Mr.
Collingwood had compiled to guide one in
following the growth of Ruskin's power of
pencil and brush, but it was a greater to
have the compiler at one's side.

As one wandered on in the way he had laid down for us our minds were first charmed by sight of the little fellow in his white frock racing with spaniel at his side, as Northcote saw him. Next grown up to be a studious lad of ten—we could in imagination see him in the schoolroom working with consummate care at his map of France. In the next year we seemed to watch him in the Herne Hill library, laughing at the humour in Cruikshanks' etchings to Grimm's famous stories, as he strove to copy them. The boy of eleven who could so minutely see and so accurately reproduce, was surely destined to excel with the pencil, and must have loved his work. One was not surprised to see the sketch of the quaint broad-roofed and picturesque wayside house at Sevenoaks which he made in the following year, 1831, upon which he has inscribed, "I believe my very first study from Nature."

A good deal has happened in the boy's life before he re-drew the set of vignettes from his sketches in North Italy. There in the little case hard by lies the precious gift that was given him on his fourteenth birthday, Rogers' *Italy*, illustrated by Turner. From that hour Turner has become a power to

the boy, and he has determined to emulate
Rogers and produce his own verses of the
Italian tour he took in 1835, and illustrate
the poem with his own pencil.

But others beside Turner have come to
his aid, and he evidently has set himself to
learn what he can from Prout. Here hangs
a wonderful bit of intricate architectural drawing which he has in the years 1833-4 copied
from his new master. There, marked No. 10
in the catalogue, is another copy of Prout,
but reduced to a miniature scale with consummate care. The lad is now fifteen, and
can go alone in matters of architectural
draughtsmanship, as witnessed by the drawing
of St. Mary's, Bristol.

In the spring of 1835 Ruskin had an attack
of pleurisy. This necessitated a whole year's
wandering on the Continent. A boy of six-
teen, he is more determined than ever to
emulate Rogers. He began his journal in
Don Juan metre, to be illustrated by pen and
pencil, and here we have from 13 to 33 a
series of the sketches which he intended for
the illustrations. In many cases he has copied
them on grey paper on a larger scale than
the originals. Originals and copies hang
side by side, and at a glance one can see

how the freshness of the touch seems to fade
in the process, and how the man whose gospel
to artists was to be that they must go to
Nature and draw what they saw, neither more
nor less, had already the gift of seeing and
being able to truthfully set forth all he saw
as he worked. Look, for example, at the
Calais Tower (13), Innspruck (29), and the
gate of the ancient palace of Nancy. But
he cannot get away from Prout, and Prout
knew nothing about mountain architecture.
Hence, while we may well gaze with wonder
at the accuracy of the outline of the Wellhorn
and Wetterhorn from the Scheideck (22), we
are obliged to admit that as yet the young
draughtsman has not felt the modelling of
mountain masses, the spirit and life of the
building of the hill, and cannot express them
with his pencil.

But it is very striking to notice how decorative his Proutesque drawing is, how fond he
is of detail. There is a quaint little sketch
of the interior of Mr. Hopkinson's carriage
(26), in which not only the humour that is
in the lad comes out, but in which his feeling
for and love of the decorative is seen in the
careful drawing of the window straps. How
much of the fine lace-like effect of rich orna-

ment was obtained by his line and dot way
of drawing with a soft pencil, is clear in this
series of 1833 sketches. But as yet it would
appear the boy has had no desire to use
colour, though it is plain from his journals and
his poems that he sees colour and delights in it.

In 1836 he makes his first essay as a
colourist. Here is a copy of a pastoral scene
with cows in foreground by Copley Fielding
(34), who became his master, and here (36) is a
cottage in Troutbeck, which he painted in the
following year, 1837. It is broad in treatment,
heavy in colour, but one sees in it the love
for purple tones which remained with him to
the end. It is quite remarkable as showing
how the influence of Copley Fielding seems
to have for the time entirely dispossessed
Prout in the young draughtsman's mind. This
is seen particularly in the sketch of Rydal
Water (40), which was one of the series he
drew whilst he was collecting material in the
Lake District for his articles on the Poetry
of Architecture, published under the *nom de
plume* of 'Kata Phusin.'

In 1840 Ruskin was threatened with phthisis,
and was taken from Oxford by his parents
to France and Italy. Here on the walls are
hung fine examples of work done by one who

was then considered to be a dying young man, by one too whose life was probably saved by the fact that his passion for drawing took him and kept him largely in the open air. As one gazes upon these from 45 to 51, the first thing that strikes one is the strength of the work, and the next that some other artist than Prout and Copley Fielding has been influencing young Ruskin. That somebody else was David Roberts, and the wonder is that the draughtsman ever came back to the delicacy of treatment which he might have sacrificed to the greater boldness and freedom he learnt from Roberts.

Yet there need not be wonder, when one comes to consider that if ever a man strove to see Truth and paint it, Ruskin was the man. This is the charm of the exhibition, we are in the Hall of Truth. There is not a single picture upon the wall from the first sketch of the boy of eleven to the last sketch of the man of sixty-four, that is not full of deep sincerity and absence of all wish to win praise or attract by other means than Truth seen and expressed.

One passes before the drawings of this series that belong to the years 1840 and 1841. One La Riccia (46), which, though it be but a pencil sketch, is aflame with sunset colour

for all who have read Ruskin's description
of the scene in the first volume of *Modern
Painters*. The other, the sketch of Castel del
Nuovo, Naples (49), where one may wonder,
as Mr. Collingwood points out in his note,
at the exquisite delicacy and feeling with which
by simple artistic artifice Ruskin varied the
monotonous windows and made the long un-
lovely street-front full of beauty and interest.

But the heart of the young wanderer yearned
not only for the long stretch of the curving
shores of Genoa, the far-off outline of the hills
beneath Vesuvius and its cloud; his was the
eye that cared for beauty of things that might
be seen and known of every cottager at home,
and here on the same wall are exhibited two
leaf studies, delicate and purposeful, drawn as
only Ruskin seems to have cared to draw them.

The hand that was busy with the first
volume of *Modern Painters* was not only
mindful of man and his work, but was con-
sidering the lilies that perish and the leaves
that fall. But his heart was where it ever was,
away among the mountains; and when he
travelled abroad next in 1845 he had in mind
not only early Florentine painting and early
Italian architecture, but mountain forms that
might serve to interpret Turner's mountain

pictures; this is well seen in his colour drawing of the background to Mesaccio's fresco of the Tribute Money (54), which was, as he tells us in *Modern Painters*, the earliest attempt on the part of an Old Master to draw mountains as they really are.

Looking upon the sketch of Florence from Fiesole (55) and the sunset at Baveno (62), one seems to perceive another style asserting itself. He has come under the influence of J. D. Harding, and from this time forward he seems to use body colour freely for his lights, and a full brush for colour, as is seen in the delightful sketch, 'The Valley of Cluses' (63). He has been working hard, too, at the study of Turner's 'Liber Studiorum'; and as one gazes at the beautiful sepia sketch of the Grande Chartreuse (66), with its inimitable arrangement of the clustered roof-trees in the near foreground, and the marvellous distances of the far valley with its winding river, one seems to see how Turner's skill has laid its enduring spell upon him.

We are carried on now for four years, to the date 1849, and see a series of studies for *Modern Painters*, vol. iii.—'The Matterhorn, 1849' (69), 'The Limetrees of Sixt' (71), and 'Aiguille Blaitière, 1849.'

One comes back again and again to these
as examples of that truth to outline, and
power to express rock-formation, that only a
devoted geologist who was a consummate
draughtsman could have compassed. He has
not cared to finish the Matterhorn sketch; all
that is left is to him supremely unimportant.
He wants the clear-cut, cruel precipice of that
mountain giant unflecked by snow, unveiled
by mist, naked and terrible. I had not seen
limestone formation more sincerely shewn than
in the sketch 'Under the Buet' (71), but the
original drawing of the 'Aiguille Blaitière'
specially claimed attention. One was enabled,
by studying this, side by side with the engraving of part of it as given, p. 188 of *Modern
Painters*, vol. iv., to give the lie direct to
those who have sometimes asserted that
Ruskin owed all the success of his illustrations to his happy choice of an engraver.
Beautiful as Armytage's work in this plate
undoubtedly is, one cannot help feeling that
it has lost by comparison a certain charm.
The drawing is more delicate and full of
expression than the plate.

The next series of drawings on the screen
and neighbouring wall from (77) to (95)
seemed to show us Ruskin's master-hand, not

RUSKIN'S BEDROOM AT BRANTWOOD.

From Photo. by Walmsley.

only as draughtsman of architectural detail, but as a colourist. They were drawings for the most part made between 1851 and 1853, and all of them were designed either to illustrate *The Stones of Venice* or to give examples of the architecture of Venice. As one stood before the 'Fondaco dei Turchi' (78) and 'Casa Dario' (83), one asked oneself whether one had ever seen colour more daringly suggestive, treatment more realistic in conveying idea of marble textures; at the same time it needed a strong magnifying glass to do justice to the separate tesserae of the gold mosaic work drawn in as background for the enrichment of the archivolt in St. Mark's (82).

But for grace and vigour and knowledge of perspective one seemed to feel that the draughtsman had reached his highest in ' The Angle of the Ducal Palace, showing the Sons of Noah' (81). As one went back in thought to the little pencil sketch of the house-front at Sevenoaks, done by the lad of twelve years old, one felt that if the whole twenty years since that time to the date of this Venetian picture had been given up to drawing, the power that here was manifest would have justified the labour.

One passed on thence to the drawings

number (105) to (106), for in these drawings,
which the reader of *Modern Painters*, vol. iv.,
chap. 2, is familiar with, one was enabled to
see the real man. At the end of the room
hung a clever copy by Arthur Severn of
Turner's famous picture, 'The Pass of Faido,
St. Gothard,' and after refreshing one's memory
of the original—exhibited so lately in London
—by a long look at this, one was able to
come back and wonder at the pains Ruskin
had taken to get at truth, and to see what it
was in the actual scene which had been the
dominant feature in Turner's mind when he
painted his imaginative transcript, and when
he added this interpretation of the spirit of the
scene to the wonder of cloudland and rock
and torrent there at the gateway of the hills.

Here, side by side with the two sketches
made on the spot between 1845 and 1855,
was the faithful copy of so much of Turner's
idealisation as was necessary for Ruskin's
purpose. There was probably no man of our
day who would have taken all this honest
pains to disentangle the real facts of the scene
from the poetic garment of praise with which
Turner had clothed them. As one came back
again and again to these Ruskin studies in
Truth, one realised more and more that this

was but an epitome of his life's aim—the secret of his success, writ in brief. Truth-seeker and Pains-taker, this little group of drawings was for him a noble monument. Close by hung Armytage's engraving of 'The Buttresses of an Alp' (109), and, near it, Ruskin's original drawing. It must have been to any but a Ruskin a quite impossible subject. To draw on so small a scale the whole of a mighty mountain side, with every fissure, each field, each belt of forest so accurately as that one could see where the foliage changed, how chestnuts gave way to beech, and beech to pine, must have appeared to other men unattemptable. But it was done here with absolute fidelity, and if the effect is not successful from the picture-maker's point of view, at least for purpose of illustrating what was meant by the passage in his writing, the end was gained. It is only right to say that in this instance it seemed the engraver's skill had indeed added to Ruskin's laborious handiwork. It was evident from such drawings of aspen and magnolia and laburnum leaves as were here, that during this time the draughtsman was keeping his hand and eye in close study and delineation of foliage. The man who could plot and plan out a whole mountain

side upon his drawing block, could also devote
days to the study of leafage and reach such
power to delineate leaf character as we find
in 'The Dryad's Crown,' an engraving of
which (138) hangs on the side wall.

We are now approaching the time between
the publication of vol. iv. and v. of *Modern
Painters*, which latter appeared in 1860.   In
the years 1858, 1859, he was evidently intent,
as Mr. Collingwood tells us, upon preparing
illustrations for a work on the history of the
chief Swiss towns.   Here on the screen are
hung examples of the work done with this
book in view.   The two most interesting ones
are 'Fribourg' (127), and 'Thun' (129).
There is for those who know these towns a
deep appeal to the historic sense as one gazes.
One seems to see why it was the towns grew
up where they did, and how they came by
their crown of tower and their fence of shining
river.   Here, too, we could not help bending
down to read a good specimen of the illustrated
letter Ruskin was in the habit of sending to
his father.   He wrote it at Säkingen on the
Rhine, and tells his father with what different
zest he is engaged now in drawing bits of
the old town to the drawing of which as a
boy he went as to a task because his father

wished it. He speaks of the deep red tulips in the cottage gardens. They shine as bright to-day at Säkingen, as I can testify, who saw them this year, but they will never shine for eyes that had such understanding of them or such joy in their cups of flame as they shone for his who penned the letter. One was glad too to see impressions made upon Ruskin's mind by the too little known Lauffenburg, a quaint Rhine town within two hours' drive of Säkingen, set in a land of blossoming orchards, and girt about by forests of dark pine. It is left to such pilgrim-seekers of truth and beauty as Ruskin to leave the main road and drop down to the bridge above the foaming torrent and hear the murmur of the waters mingle with the hum of the market folk. Lauffenburg is too little visited.

On the second screen are examples of his work in full colour and pencil done in Switzerland in the early sixties, and specimens of his finest architectural work from the Abbeville series, 1868, and Verona, 1869.

We stop before the well-known chromolithographic reproduction of a portrait of himself by his own hand drawn in 1864 (156). One gazes at the wistful, tenderly, thoughtful face of the blue-eyed man, and then at the grey-haired, saddened sage who sits, life's labours done, in his Brantwood study, as painted for us in 1897 by W. G. Collingwood, and as one contrasts the portraits, one cannot help the thought that the sorrow and pain that wrought more change in it than the passing years did, was borne for us men and for our helping.

One little jewel of a sketch claims particular attention; it is the daintiest piece of work imaginable, entitled 'On the Reuss below Lucerne.' We pass on, and our eyes are attracted by a marvellous bit of colour—an Australian opal drawn by him to illustrate opaline qualities of light and lustre for a mineralogical lecture. A man near by said, a little contemptuously: "Oh, that's just a trick." Yes, it was just a trick, but it took a Ruskin forty years of constant endeavour to see rightly and to draw exactly to learn the trick; and it is the most astonishing piece of living colour and light in the whole collection.

There are on the same screen specimens of his Verona work, the most interesting being the pencil sketch of Can Grande on horseback (169). One positively feels more wind in the saddle-cloth than one felt as one gazed at the original marble, and this is saying much.

But the picture that most interested me was a swift sketch of the Rialto in water-colour, done one morning before breakfast, in 1870. Here for the first time in the whole collection does one seem to see Ruskin letting himself go, and indulging in the delight of less restrained impressionism. He seems here to be laying on colour for pure joy, and giving reins to the natural desire he so combated of painting for effect.

It is as masterly in its accuracy of drawing as it is forcible in colour, and it allows one to know what Ruskin could have done if instead of drawing with an earnest purpose as a teacher, he had simply proposed to indulge himself in the delights of dream and colour for fame and praise.

We cannot pass by the series of sketches on the wall, of studies made to help the students in the Drawing School at Oxford in 1871 without noticing the care which he gave to the right delineation of so simple a thing as a candle. The humble 'short eight' becomes in his tender and true hands, a thing of beauty, I expect of marvel also, to his Oxford students.

On the back of the last screen are examples of his drawings during the last ten years of 'the Master's working life.' Here a pencil sketch of the Glacier des Bossons (195) drawn in 1874, with such fidelity that one not only seems to realise the glacier's flow, but to observe how it clings to the mountain slope above which it travels.   There a fine drawing of the Casa Foscari (197), here a forcible drawing of Gershom's Dog from the famous Botticelli fresco in the Sistine Chapel.   It is not only the dog that interests one, so full of life and go and bark and bite that one is glad Gershom has it well under his arm, but one sees how with the faithfulness of the fresco-painter himself Ruskin has reproduced the fine embroidery on the purple sleeve of the young man.   In 1882 we are taken by the draughtsman to Lucca, and we have the delicate detail of the carvings and marble inlay of a pier in the porch of San Martino brought before us (209).

We leave architectural detail and wonder at the daintiness and truth with which Ruskin can paint heather (218), or moss, or fern (219), or draw to the life the breast-plume of a peacock (220), or the rays of the same plume, enlarged five times for our better learning.

But it is not delicacy alone of which, in feather-drawing, he is master.   There, in the 'eagle's wing,' from the sculpture on the Hospital of St. John the Evangelist, at Venice

(203), one realises how strength as well as delicacy is part of the cunning of hand.

We are drawing to the close of Ruskin's days of draughtsmanship. The cloud of ill-health is settling down upon him. There, numbered (213), hangs a remembrance of his last journey across the border to the land of his fathers. The slight sketch of Traquhair, 1883, done on an envelope for want of better material handy to him, completes the exhibition, as the biographical history of the collection.

We turn back to the 'Morning Cloud on the Coniston Old Man' (206) as he saw it in 1877 ; we think of the many mornings that he, earliest arisen of all the dwellers by the lake, saw the cloud lift and felt his own life little better than a cloud that vanisheth. We think of the sadness as the cloud fell on him, of the gladness as it lifted, and know that somewhere beyond the falling or the lifting of any earthly cloud, this seeker of Truth and setter forth of Sincerity by pencil or by pen, has surely entered rest, and knows his work was not in vain, in the land where the true light shines, and life and love and truth and praise are for everlasting.

It is for students of Ruskin a great matter to have had the chance of seeing this exhibi-

tion. His artist mind and its growth, his aim
and desire, the sincerity of his heart and hand
could not otherwise have been made so clear to
them. Impressive in its simple appeal to do
good work and love good work when we see it,
it is a tonic and an inspiration to all who will
thoughtfully visit it. But the book is too soon
to be closed, and this it is that may justify the
record of it. There were many voices in the
room that bade us stay—many pictures that
seem to call us back for one more look, but we
were bent on seeing Brantwood once more.

The sky was cloudless azure, the hills bathed
in sunshine, as we rowed with our kindest of
guides across the lake for a last look at 'The
Master's home.' Whitely shone the Thwaite
behind us, whitely shone out Brantwood in
front of us, and passing along under Coniston
Bank Ground, it was easy to see what absolute
privacy the forethought of Mrs. Severn had
obtained for the Master when she became
possessor of this adjacent property. From
Coniston Bank all the way up the breast of the
woody fell, away beyond Lawson Park and
the larch plantations that backed it to the
south, every inch of the ground was now in the
Brantwood demesne from the lake margin to
the sky line.

We landed at the little dock which Ruskin's undergraduate friends had helped to hollow out. There lay the 'Jumping Jenny' just as she lay in the days when she served the Master. I could not help thinking that she felt her enforced idleness, her very paintlessness gave her a look of sorrow. A daughter of the household, sitting as in some old picture with her sewing maid beside her beneath the shadow of the sycamore, welcomed us ashore, and bade us go up through the garden and wander into the house at will. So up the steps and through the single sunflowers, and the sweet peas, and the young standard apple-trees that were set as a kind of fence against the emerald field right and left of it, we passed ; we crossed the road, we went up by the lodge and by the barn out-house, where the republican press once used to work, and could not help standing for a moment to make out in the rough-cast and stucco, the words that Linton had left in graffiti to posterity there, which bade us in classic Latin remember that to 'will is to do.' I noted how, though the dove-cot had cut the inscription 'God and the People' in twain, the birds of peace and love cooed their blessing to the sentiment. On through the backyard, and under the 'high sounding portico,' the arch that seems to tunnel the whole house it up-shoulders to give access to the front, we moved, and found ourselves at the simple, unpretending entrance. Years ago the blue-eyed professor had come from that doorway with a smile, and with hands outstretched in welcome. Now he could not come. But on entering all seemed as if he must still be within. There, fronting us, hung the Burne Jones sketches of Cressida, calm with the mulberry twig and the sword, and Cleopatra, leaning forward with look of fear and hate, her feet among the frogs that croak below.

But it was to the study that one instinctively turned for memories of the Master of the house. Entering it, one almost expected to see him rise from the table in the little bay window, where so often he had watched the rising sun strike on the summit of the Old Man and light the lawns of Coniston. There was the chair, there too the quaint inkstand and the two bronze candlesticks, but the writer had passed away.

One glance round the walls. The tender little Passover-scene that Rossetti drew, was in its place; Joseph was striking the blood upon the lintel, and touching the hand of the boy Jesus; the blood was flowing down one

of the two sideposts ; there was the blot or
blur in the background where the lamb, as
Rossetti designed it, was being slain for sacrifice.
That blotting out of the lamb is surely eloquent
for ever of the tender heart of Ruskin that could
not and would not endure the sight. Then
one's eyes went across the desk in mid-room,
whereon were the porphyries, minerals, crystals, agates, and precious stones, to that
exquisite drawing of the façade of Lucca
Cathedral which his own hand had wrought.
Caught back for a moment to note the old
xiv. century Bible lying where it always lay
for his daily reading, again our eyes fell upon
the bow-window and the table and the vacant
chair, and one remembered how the last time
one had seen him he was sitting by that table,
not any longer with pen in hand, but with
his long beard falling to the table, his hands
quietly clasped in front of him, and his eyes
gazing intently upon the wild flowers in the
vase before him.

Now there was no need of any ministry of
flowers. He had done with these things. But
one flower bloomed on upon the study wall.
There, above the fireplace, the lily-maiden of
God, the rose of the world, knelt, as Luca
Della Robbia had dreamed she knelt, before

her infant Child, and the white cherub faces
with looks of joyous adoration gleamed against
the blue-enamelled background of the beautiful
terra-cotta. Flanking this tender work of art
were the Cypriote pots that Cesnola had un-
earthed. Greyish yellow in colour, with their
circle within circles in black or red upon them,
it seemed as if the old sun-worshippers had
been brought to the feet of the daystar for all
the world, and as if for all the shadow of
death, the little study was too full of light, too
full of desire that would bid the light grow on
to a more perfect day to make us feel the
dark.

We moved back to the window to gaze upon
the scene Ruskin loved best. There up the
lake shone the house that gave him ever welcome and the joy of sympathy. Beyond it
Yewdale Crag and Raven Crag stood up with
their everlasting question, " How came we to
be here ?" Nearer in the north-west Wetherlam, above Long Crags, melted into the
Coniston Range, and the village lay beyond
the blue grey water-plain on the green and
sunny slope of the skirts of the Old Man. That
slope seemed far up above the village to divide
and give an entrance into the far recesses of
the hills ; a white torrent foamed from the

height down towards the mountain gate and either side the portals of the recess stood the crags; the one Ruskin used to call Lion Crag, the other Tiger Crag. Above Lion Crag, which is certainly a more poetic name than Scrow, rose up a conical green hill which men call 'The Bell,' but which Ruskin re-named St. George's Hill.

My eyes went from the hill of St. George, which I hope may one day find its new name in the ordnance sheet, up to the height of Coniston Old Man and down to the levels of the mere. I had never observed before how large and fair an Alp as distinct from the Coniston Range lay between us and the mountains to the west, nor had one realised how entirely this Alp had been subdued by the plow, how full of the labour of men's hands, such labour as Ruskin had ever glorified, was that quiet pastoral scene which every morn made new for the Master's eyes.

We left the window and passed out of the study that had been the fountain of so much thought to help our time. A friend at my side said as he went out, "I don't know what it is, but I found I could not speak above a whisper. It was just like being in church." So with hushed voices we went to the dining-room.

It is a room filled with light from the south
and west, and its walls are full of voices of the
past. There, over the fireplace, hangs the
great Venetian Doge from Titian's half-con-
sumed canvas, and the Annunciation by
Tintoret. To the left Turner looks at us
wistfully as he looked once in a mirror at
himself, when, as a boy, he attempted his own
portraiture. On the eastern wall above the
sideboard may be seen bits of marble that
Andrea the Pisan once sculptured for the font
of Philip de Medici. But one forgets these
in the interest of looking at the little lad in
white frock and blue sash running by the
side of the King Charles spaniel, as Northcote
drew him in the year 1822, for that fair-haired
and blue-eyed child is John Ruskin. There
is nothing in the child face that makes one
feel presage of future greatness. "A simple
child that lightly draws its breath" and
enjoys his scamper with the dog, that is all
we see.

Right and left of him hang the portraits of
his father and mother. The father swift of eye,
earnest, gentle, and thoughtful. The mother
keen of face and managing, at least that is the
impression her clever face made upon one as
one gazed. But the face of her, once seen,

RUSKIN'S STUDY AT BRANTWOOD.

From Photo. by Walmsley.

does not admit of its being forgotten. I see it clearly as I write.

We left the dining-room and entered the drawing-room. It was changed somewhat; the Turners I had remembered on the walls were no longer there, but the same quaint old-fashioned protest against 'greenery yallery, Grosvenor gallery' paper furnishings was in evidence. Ruskin's copy of Jochebed from Botticelli's fresco balanced on the eastern wall the glorious fair Rosamond by Burne Jones. On the south wall above the bookcase hung the forcible sunset Holman Hunt drew as he saw it glorious over the plains of Troy.

We turned and left the room, thinking of one who was beyond all sun-setting, for whom no more the darkness follows day, and so away from the house with just one pause half-way down the drive. In that pause one realised how humble was the little cottage dwelling of which Ruskin became possessor in 1872, and what changes the poets who were before him would find if their souls came this way.

Out of the gate we went, that gate where he had in earlier years stood to say farewell, the gate that must now open and close upon us without speeding voice. It is the last time we shall hear the gate clang behind us. The book

H

of Brantwood is closed for ever.   There beyond
the tree tops to the north, high up in middle
sky, lies the dip in the mountain range that
gives entrance into Cumberland.   We must
seek the mountain gateway; we shall seek it
sadly to-night, so much of the heart of us must
here remain, here in our vale of sacred memories,
here in his vale of labour and of rest.

CHAPTER V.

RUSKIN AND THE HOME ART INDUSTRIES IN THE LAKE DISTRICT.

ONE of the many rememberable talks with the Professor in old Oxford and Hinksey digging days, turned on the question of how to add happiness to the country labourer's lot. His eyes flashed and his voice rose with its earnest sing-song as he urged that it was the simple duty of every squire and every clergyman to see that idle hands should have something found for them to do by other than the Devil ; and that it was a scandal that the church had neither rest homes or recreation rooms nor public houses where the poor might find cheer and solace without the necessity of drink on the long winter evenings. " I know," he said, " that a certain number of wholly good and earnest evangelical lords and ladies do erect mission rooms on their estates, but though a

good Bible Lesson is interesting enough, a bad
one is very poor stuff, and the poor need to
be taught how to enjoy themselves and not
to be preached at. The gospel that needs
preaching is not how to get to heaven by
swallowing wholesale certain church or chapel
doctrines, but how to make earth heaven by
doing certain fair deeds. And it has always
seemed to me," he added, " that your most
earnest preachers of to-day have deliberately
refused to tell the people that God did not
make their misery nor does He desire they
should continue in it, that what He desires
is their health and utmost happiness here and
hereafter. And that it is possible, if people
will be content with the gifts an all-loving
Father gives them, to find here and now in
the humblest life an abundance of both. Why
don't the bishops admonish their clergy to
see to it that side by side with parish church
and parish mission room there shall be a
parish workshop, where the blacksmith and
the village carpenter shall of a winter evening
teach all the children who will be diligent and
will learn, the nature of iron and wood, and
the use of their eyes and hands.

I would have the decoration of metal and
wood brought in later, and these children as

they grow shall feel the joy of adding ornament to simple surfaces of metal or wood ;
but always they shall be taught the use of
the pencil, and the delight of close observation
of flower in the field and bird in the hedgerow and animal in the wild wood. We must
bring joy, the joy of eye and hand-skill
to our cottage homes." In some such words
did the Professor talk, and his words were
not forgotten. It had been my fortune to
come under the teaching of Edward Thring,
himself a student of Ruskin's theories. I had
learned at Uppingham that if a boy was not
gifted with power of language or mathematics,
nor likely to prove a good classic, he was not
on that account to be despaired of by his
headmaster. At least he might be clever with
his hands, and I once heard Thring say that
one of the proud moments of his life was when
he saw the old archdeacon's schoolroom, that
had done its classical work since the days of
great Elizabeth, turned into a carpenter's shop,
and loud with the hammer and the saw.

It was not to be wondered at that when
one came into the lake country and settled
down to the care of the little village of Wray
on Windermere, one of the first things one
should seek for was to find how to help the

joy of the winter evenings in the cottages. There were really no poor among the people, but there was plenty of time for training hands to the wood-carver's art. Song was already one of the features of the village life ; the postmaster was a musician. The old spinning-wheel days were spoken of tenderly by the village grandmothers, but the thought of reviving that industry never occurred to one as possible. Wood-carving was possible, and friends at Grasmere were as keen for it as we were at Wray ; some also at Ambleside were wishful to learn. To make a long story short, a lady was engaged to come down from South Kensington to give a course of lessons in the three villages, and our humble home industry in the lake district was set on foot.

The last winter we were at Wray my wife began to make experiments in metal repoussé work stimulated by the amateur efforts of a friend who chanced to call one day—and in the hope of turning such knowledge to account in our own village or elsewhere. There hangs before me as I write, the first dish she made, her tools being I think a hammer and a French nail.

We were encouraged in the possibility of teaching this art to unskilled hands by the efforts made by a Swiss butler at Croft, my mother-in-law's house, who after one or two lessons set to work on an intricate pattern my wife gave him of a scroll from a Florentine 'scaldino' and who produced an effective bit of decoration. I like to think of this man's experiment as part of the seed from which our Keswick School of Industrial Arts sprang.

Circumstances brought us over the Raise gap into Cumberland in 1883 ; we left behind the wood-carvers in Westmoreland, but not the sense of brightness in their cottage homes which the interest of this simple handicraft had added. We left behind the presence of the Master, and the possibility of going over the Hawkshead Hill to talk with him at Brantwood from time to time of the work. We carried with us his wishes and his hopes for the evangel of home industries. The Langdale spinning-wheels had just begun to hum ; we had none to help Cumberland homes in this way, but at least we knew something of the elements of wood-carving and metal repoussé work, and we were amongst a people who must necessarily have little work to do out of the tourist season, and were in a town which had none of the excitements of the 'threepenny theatre' or 'penny-gaff' to act

as counter attraction. Besides the town was
a Viking town. Town of the wyke of Ketel
the Dane; and these Vikings were living
here still, with probably the same aptitude for
wood-carving and wood-shaping, and with that
same love of ornament that their forefathers
had brought with them, who came with Ingolf
and Thorolf from over the sea,—supplemented,
as I suppose, by the love of it that the
German colony of miners in the days of
Queen Elizabeth had in their hearts. It
was true that there was no evidence of
its existence in the cottages, unless the
raddle mark and whitening pattern on hearth
or door-stone might be looked upon as
survivals of a day of Scandinavian ornament; but some one had evidently been fond
of wood-carving of old, for not a settle nor
high 'seat-post' nor meal-ark or kist in the
older farms but had careful scroll and vine-
roll ornament upon them, dating some of these
from King James' time, and the later Restor-
ation down to the middle of last century. There
was evidence here that the love of wood-
carving detail was cared for in Cumberland
homes. Some of the patterns on these meal-
arks were clearly Norse, the linked serpent
was sign of it, others showed an earlier origin

and told of the time when the forefathers of these dalesmen were still dwellers in the land of the palm, Aryans in their eastern home. The conventionalised palm-roll on the Cumberland furniture has often set me thinking of the permanency of traditional ornament among a pastoral people. But this is by the way.

Here then at Keswick was just the place for an experiment in home industries. A little country town, dull enough in winter evenings, lacking enough in work and wages of all year round besides, and full enough of tourists in a summer season to ensure a sale for the goods made. So we set to work in the winter of 1883-4, called a committee together, enlisted the help of a gentleman in the neighbourhood who was an artist and designer, and engaging a teacher of wood-carving from the South Kensington School, offered her services to the ladies of the neighbourhood on such terms during the day as enabled us to hold a class free of charge for working-men and lads during the evening. We met in the Parish room three nights a week, my wife superintending the brass repoussé work, and a clever local jeweller making experiments as to the manipulation of the sheet metal in the

matter of beating it up into shape from the
flat.   Within a month of the start we could
produce very simple brass or copper finger
plates for doors which found a sale.   Our
expenses of that first session of five months
amounted to £181, but we had produced work
which we estimated to be worth £118.   Our
expenses were kept as low as possible.   The
parish room in which for the first ten years the
classes were held was lent us, and though it was
a very considerable trouble to have to clear
away all benches and tools at the end of each
evening's work, the workers cheerily undertook
this, for the room was quite certain to be needed
for parochial work on the following day.   For
the second winter session we engaged a clever
wood-carver to come once a week from Carlisle,
and the sum of £9—the only sum ever asked
for of the neighbourhood to help to defray
expenses—was collected.   The working expenses
of this second season was £147.   A local
exhibition of work done was held at Easter
in the Town Hall, and I remember well the
astonishment on the faces of some of the
townsmen who found that this work had been
done in their midst by men and lads whom
they knew well enough in any capacity but
that of wood or metal-worker.

At the third session, 1886, we found applications were so numerous for admission to the school that we could afford to be careful in our selection, and could impose such rules as that no lad should be admitted to work till he could prove by attendance at the drawing class his ability to trace his pattern for himself on to the metal or wood. From the first we had wished to see each metal-worker finish his work throughout, but the difficulty of having proper accommodation in a smith's shop prevented this. Nevertheless as time went on we fitted up an iron room, hard by the parish room, with concrete floor, blow-pipe, anvil, vices and the like ; and one of the cleverest of our School hands thenceforward undertook to teach himself as he went along and to teach others as he worked. At the end of the third session we found ourselves with our expenditure doubled but our sales had doubled also, and we were possessed of assets that showed us we were £131 to the good. The experiment so far had shewn itself entirely self-supporting, and from that day to this it has not looked back.

For ten years we worked in the parish room under great inconveniences. Then our committee determined to obtain a site and build workshops and show-room, office and designer's

room in one, and while the School itself out of
its earnings contributed £300 and the County
Council £200, friends to the enterprise contributed the balance of the £800 necessary, and
in 1894 we entered into possession of as
compact and picturesque a School of Art as
may be found in Great Britain. For the
design of the School we were indebted to
Messrs. Paley & Austin, of Lancaster. Amongst
those who had helped us were Walter Crane,
Holman Hunt, and that truest champion of
the whole movement, our dear old friend G. F.
Watts, the Royal Academician.

But the spirit that had made the whole
venture possible, was the spirit of him whose
face hangs now upon its walls, the spirit of
John Ruskin.

Most visitors go to see the pencil works near
Greta Hall, some are glad to see Southey's
home upon the tree-clad hill hard by; it is
but a step beyond in the direction of Crosthwaite Church, and the eyes of all who cross
Greta Bridge will light on a pleasant building
swathed in flowers, with balcony such as might
be welcomed by the spinners of old time, with
chimneys just such as those round chimneys on
their square pedestals which Wordsworth so
much admired, and which Ruskin himself

delighted to draw. Beneath the balcony runs
a legend,

"The loving eye and skilful hand
Shall work with joy and bless the land."

I once heard a tourist spell it out to his
friend and say, "Oh yes, it's the Keswick eye
hospital, you know." And truly it is an eye
hospital if by that is meant an institution for
getting men to use their eyes and see beauty in
living design and the worth of a springing curve.

Enter the garden gate, climb up the round of
stone steps, pass along the balcony, and we find
ourselves at a door leading into the Show
Room of the Keswick School of Industrial
Arts, upon whose front is a tablet with the
words from Browning,

"Oh earth as God has made it all is beauty,
And knowing this is love and love is duty;"

as one lifts one's eyes to the hills from that
balcony, or entering into the Show Room and
crossing to the further side one gazes out upon
the ample mead, the winding river, the distant
hills, the flashing lake, one feels, unless one's
heart is stone, that Browning is right.

Here is the ideal craftsman's home of work,
and here in the winter months, the windows
gleam and, as one passes, one hears above the

sound of Greta swirling by, the sound of the
anvil and the chink of the hammers, and
passing on may find a set of men as proud
of their school as they are well behaved and
courteous.   Men who scorn all that is meant
by the word drink, and men who, though many
of them live laborious days, will not miss if they
can help it crowning the labour of the day with
the rest of this complete change of work for
hand and eye.

You will find the lady who started it all
faithfully at her post no matter what the
weather is, noting and criticising each piece
of work, and deciding if it shall be passed
and have the School stamp—a lozenge with
the initials K.S.I.A. upon it.   You will find
another lady the friend and confidante of all
the workers from the first, giving out or taking
in the work and paying for it its just value
to the worker.   You will see the Art Director
planning with sure hand how this or that
metal problem is to be met.   You will pass
into the next room and mingle with the wood-
carvers round their teacher, or on another
evening you will watch the men with pencil
in hand doing what they may to reproduce
a branch of wild rose upon their drawing
boards, or modelling a cast of a leaf in clay

beneath the direction of their drawing teacher. You will open a door and find yourself in another room odorous with pitch and hissing loud as the red-hot bowl is tempered for its twentieth time. This is the abode of Vulcan and Aeolus *pro tem.* The stithy is being arranged for outside. Iron work has in this last year of the century been added to the copper and brass work. Passing through this room you will enter the workshop where silver work goes forward, and beyond may chance to find an enameller's gas-stove red hot and a worker in enamel busy.

But in summer you will note that the chief attraction is the Show Room, and as you gaze at the varied wares of wood, of brass, of copper, of silver, and of electro-plate, you will not be surprised to learn that the amount of work turned out annually is estimated at £1700, and that the difficulty is rather not how to dispose of the work done but how to keep customers in good temper while they are waiting for their order in its due rotation to be executed.

And what really is the worth of the School work? It cannot be estimated in pounds. Go to the homes of any of the workers. Ask their wives or their brothers and you shall learn. Go to any of the workers themselves and you shall learn that the good of the School to them has been that they now have always something to turn to on a dull evening and something that has opened their eyes to see what they used to pass by without notice in flower life and bird life, and beauty of light and shade, of cloud and sunshine, upon the fellside of their native vale.

But if you were to ask the Art Director, I think he would say that he is astounded at the natural refinement that has come upon the men ; a coarse word, a vulgar suggestion is not known in the School. He would say further that he realises here in this little School at Keswick, something of the guild camaraderie of the olden time. If a man finds out any secret in working metal he does not care to keep it to himself, it is at once at the service of all his fellow-workers. It is this spirit that is better than rubies, whose price is above silver and gold.

And if you were to enquire of the townsmen what they thought of the institution, I believe the more thoughtful would answer, "We know nothing of the ideal before the mind of the promoters, this we know, that it is the grandest temperance agent in the place."

Now to whom is this owed? Whose is the spirit that inspired it? There is only one answer possible, it is the mind and spirit of John Ruskin. How well I remember the day when we took our first little results of brass repoussé over to Brantwood to talk about the work in the spring of 1884. How pleased he was to hear about it all. How grieved he was to think that we should allow our workers to work in a mixed metal. Copper yes, gold yes, silver yes, but this *brass* was neither fish, flesh, nor good fresh herring. It was a base alloy. And yet though he clapped his hands over it, and vowed it was shockingly immoral, he admitted the work was careful and true, and was forced to allow that much of the sunshine that dazzled the eyes of the heroes of Homer's song, was just this brass, this base alloy on shining threshold and on glittering helm. Ruskin was too enfeebled in health to admit of our troubling him afterwards with details of our work, but he knew of our progress, and rejoiced in it, and from time to time sent tender messages to the School.

In Wordsworth's *Guide to the Lakes*, written in 1810, the poet speaks sadly of the "unfortunate alterations in the circumstances of

I

the native peasantry at the English lakes from
a cause which began to operate about the time
when visitors first began to come as tourists
to the lakes, and was being felt in every
house."

"The *Estatesmen* had—he tells us—up to
this time profits from two sources, their flocks
and the home manufactures by their women
and children of the produce of their flocks.
'They spun their own wool in their own
houses (work chiefly done in the winter season)
and carried it to market for sale. But,' adds
the poet, 'by the invention and universal
application of machinery this second resource
has been cut off, the gains being so far
reduced as not to be sought after but by a
few aged persons disabled from other employment.'"

Wordsworth saw that the introduction of
machinery had increased manufacturing enterprise, and that this in turn had quickened
agricultural industries, but he adds, " This is
far from making amends; the productive
women and child labour at home has ceased,
and in consequence the proprietors and farmers
being no longer able to maintain themselves
upon small farms, several are united into one
and the buildings go to decay or are destroyed;

or the lands of the *estatesmen* being mortgaged and the owners constrained to part with them, they fall into the hands of wealthy purchasers who in like manner unite and consolidate." In a word the spinning-wheel had ceased to hum at the cottage door and the estatesman was vanishing from the land.

That Wordsworth knew what he was talking about is plain from the note he appended to that sonnet he wrote in 1819 on the Spinning-wheel, which begins,

"Grief thou hast lost an ever ready friend
Now that the cottage Spinning-wheel is mute."

"I could write," he says, "a treatise of lamentation upon the changes brought about amongst the cottages of Westmoreland by the silence of the Spinning-wheel. During long winter nights and wet days the wheel upon which wool was spun gave employment to a great part of the family. The old man, however infirm, was able to card the wool as he sate in a corner by the fireside, and often when a boy have I admired the cylinders of carded wool which were softly laid upon each other at his side. Two wheels were often at work on the same floor; and others of the family—chiefly little children—were occupied in teasing and cleaning the wool to fit it for

the hand of the carder.   So that all except the
smallest infants were contributing to the mutual
support.

Such was the employment that prevailed in
the pastoral dales.   Where wool was not at
hand in the small rural towns, the wheel for
spinning flax was almost in constant use, if
knitting was not preferred, which latter occupation has the advantage (in some cases dis-
advantage) that not being from necessity
stationary, it allowed of gossiping about from
house to house, which good wives reckoned an
idle thing."

This habit of the congregating for spinning
and gossip was not confined to Westmoreland,
for I have heard our old sexton at Crosthwaite
tell of how when he was 'a laal lad' he was
mostly about yance a week told off to laate his
mother's wheel at yan nebbor's cottage and
carry it to tudder for spinnin' neet.   This was
at Wythburn in the good old days.

But it was not only to the content and
comfort of the households that the spinning-
wheel till the end of the last century contributed, it added to the picturesqueness of
the estatesman's home also.   Anyone who
remembers the picturesque gallery and over-
hanging eaves of the farm at Monk Coniston,

of the well-roofed entrances and stairway land-
ings or balconies of the houses at Hawkshead,
of the farm house at Smethwaite Bridge near
great Howe, and one or two of the more
ancient houses on the Borrodale road and at
the entrance of the courts at Keswick, will
understand how the need of sitting out of doors
in our long twilight evenings of April and May,
or in the rainy weather throughout the year to
go on with the business of the spinning-wheel
made these balconies or galleries an imperative
and natural addition to house architecture in
the Lake District.

It was to these spinning balconies and large
eaved shelters for the spinsters that so much
of the picturesqueness of old Cumberland and
Westmoreland farmsteads was owed.   It is
probable that the ample porches which were of
old time such a feature of our dale cottages
were in part the resultant of a need for accommodation for the good wife and her wheel.

The folklore of the spinning-wheel has ceased
from out the land, but in that inimitable *Song
for the Spinning-wheel* which Wordsworth wrote,

> "Swiftly turn the murmuring wheel
> Night has brought the welcome hour
> When the weary fingers feel
> Help as if from faery power,"

one fragment of it remains immortal. It was a belief in Grasmere that when the sheep were sleeping on the fell, the wheel went more merrily and the spindles ran more true :

> "Now beneath the starry sky,
>   Couch the widely scattered sheep,
>   Ply the pleasant labour, ply!
>   For the spindle, while they sleep
>   Runs with speed more smooth and fine
>   Gathering up a trustier line."

That song was composed for Mary Hutchinson, and as one writes, Greta Hall, where she sometimes abode as Southey's amanuensis, is before my eyes. I am sitting in the spinner's porch of the cottage of St. George,—house sacred to the last memories of the ancient Radcliffe family,—house consecrate to present memories of the founder of the Guild of St. George, John Ruskin. As one listens one can hear the hum of the treadle and the click, click of the loom, and if Wordsworth who once resided as a boy in this Keswick vale with a good dame in her humble cottage, and later, grown to manhood was nigh being tempted to become a scientist and a chemist at Windebrow and a constant dweller in the valley, could now come along, he would pause here for sheer pleasure to hear a sound he so much loved, and would be glad to know that the words of lament in his *Guide to the Lakes* had not fallen on deaf ears, and that followers of the last true poet of the Lakes, John Ruskin, had brought back into being the music and the melody of wheel and spindle to be the joy and the solace of northern homes. If he had entered the house he would have found it filled with the products of the said loom and spindle. Not harden-sark as of old, nor blue bed-gown material truly, but honestly hand-spun and hand-woven linen, grey as the skies are grey, or golden yellow as the waving larches upon Latrigg-side.

The old poet would have been a little surprised to learn that the embroideries upon the linen are worked with threads dyed into glow of rose and green and gold in a factory at Cockermouth within sight of his own nursery window, and I can believe he would have wondered what fine ladies could be found hereabout—from princesses downward—to deck themselves in rainbow hues, and wear Greek and Sicilian laces wrought in Cumberland; but of this truly I am sure, he would have fallen to question as to how the spinning-wheel, so long silent, had been made again to hum its simple air, and he would learn that it was Ruskin's deed of mercy to his age and

Ruskin's heart of grace that brought this wonder to pass.

The history of the reintroduction of a dead art into the cottage homes of Westmoreland and Cumberland is a fairy story and for Ruskin's sake it should be told.

We are here at St. George's Cottage at the fountain-head of information, for Miss Twelves who lives here was the person who practically carried out the work first in Langdale and afterwards here in Keswick. It is plain as one looks round the walls of the quaint 16th century cottage to see who was the inspirer of the work. There hangs a photograph of Ruskin, here a little bit of an illuminated psalter with the words, "Prosper Thou the work of our hands upon us : prosper Thou our handiwork," the original of which was a Brantwood treasure. The motto 'To-day' is seen on one wall and a photograph of the Pall for the Master's coffin which was woven here and worked at the adjacent Keswick School of Industrial Arts hangs upon another.

But the hand that turned this reader of *Fors Clavigera*, this warm-hearted enthusiast for the Master into the channel of its endeavour, whose was it? It was the hand of *Fors*. As chance would have it, when a young lawyer

MISS TWELVES COTTAGE AT CROSTHWAITE, KESWICK.

from Broxbourne came into tenancy of his lonely dwelling at Neaum Crag above Elterwater, he invited Miss Twelves to come up from the south to help him to arrange his house and to engage his servants, and act when his summer guests were with him as good genius of the household, and in his winter absence as neighbourly caretaker. And again as *Fors* would have it, there stood in the inglenook of the drawing-room a certain ancient spinning-wheel more for ornament and the echoes of an earlier day than anything else. But the visitors in that summer of 1883 at the Crag would often touch the treadle and wish they knew how to spin, and the host, Mr. Albert Fleming, remembered Wordsworth's sonnet on the spinning-wheel, and had a heart that was able to feel for the sorrows of those brave, independent, proud-natured, old dames still to be found in many a cottage of Westmoreland and Cumberland who were willing to work, but could not beg, and who often spoke to him of the grand old days when a poor widowed body might still look with cheer to the morrow, knowing that all the wool she could spin into yarn had market value. One such old body in her 87th year lived just below the Crag at Skelwith Bridge,

Grasmere, and as soon as she saw the old wheel her face brightened and the aged fingers moved for all their age, as if they had become young again, and the wheel went round, and the line ran, and spinning in Westmoreland had again begun.

But there was the question of how to get more wheels. Miss Twelves and Mr. Fleming ransacked Westmoreland, but no wheels were forthcoming, or only such as were in fragments or hopelessly out of gear. A wheel was obtained from the Isle of Man. It was a gracious gift of that ancient island mother to make some amends for the harrying of our lake-land homes in Viking times of long ago. At Skelwith Bridge lived a clever carpenter and bobbin turner, and incited to the task by the enthusiasm of the wheel-finders and 'fettlers,' and with such suggestions as the dames who had spun when they were children could supply, the carpenter, Fleming, and the bobbin-turner, Coward, contrived between them to make twelve new wheels.

There appeared a letter in *The Standard* of that October, giving an account of the revival of spinning at the English lakes. The writer of it sent a copy to Brantwood. It cheered Mr. Ruskin's heart, and won for the promoters of the industry, the master's friendship and constant interest in the work.

Ruskin speaks of this in the last volume of *Fors*. He is writing a year after the inception of the project in October, 1884, after describing the intended uses of a room at the Sheffield Museum for the illustration of all that Athene and Penelope would approve. " The mystery of the 'divine spiral' from finest to firmest, which renders lace possible at Valenciennes, anchorage possible after Trafalgar—the mystery of weaving, 'the eternal harmony of warp and woof,' and the accomplished phase of needle-work." He adds, " Very thankfully I can now say that this vision of thread and needlework, though written when my fancy had too much possession of me, is now being in all its branches realised by two greatly valued friends, the spinning on the old spinning-wheel with most happy and increasingly acknowledged results systematized here among our West-moreland Fells by Albert Fleming, the useful sewing by Miss Stanley of Whitelands College."

The idea that Mr. Fleming conceived, which was worked out by Miss Twelves, was, that all who were willing among the older and needier of the neighbourhood should come down to a pretty little cottage by Elterwater tarn that had stood in its simple peace beside the laughing streamlet from the fell, for more than two hundred years. This, in memory of the clothing of the destitute by the good Saint of Amiens, was appropriately called ' St. Martin's,' and there they should learn again the art of spinning. Thence, having so learned it, they should take the wheels to their cottages and return their bobbins full of spun-thread at a price. The flax was obtained from Belfast, and the pay was to be 2s. a lb. for the spun article, increasing of course in proportion as the thread spun became more fine. Christmas Eve, 1883, at the Crag, saw the first gathering of the would-be spinsters, and Easter Day of 1884 saw the first piece of linen upon the St. Martin's loom hand-spun and hand-woven in Langdale for two generations. I have often heard Miss Twelves tell of how Giotto helped them to rig up that loom in St. Martin's. Little enough could the great Florentine, as he designed or worked with his own hands at the weaver's panel in his splendid Duomo tower, have imagined that, centuries after, his stone picture of an Italian home-industry would come to the aid of Norse peasants in a far-off Westmoreland vale, and be the means of giving a new lease of life to a dead industry in British homes.

After long quest the loom or its component parts was found in the cellar of a Kendal manufacturer, and brought with triumph to St. Martin's ; but joy was turned to sadness to find that none knew how the parts should be put together again. The dale-priest, who was keenly interested in the revival of the industry, came and shook his head, the oldest inhabitants looked in, but could not 'mind on,' and at the last, as *Fors* would have it, Miss Twelves remembered that a friend at Ambleside had the series of photographs of panels on Giotto's famous Campanile, and a messenger was despatched post-haste to borrow them. So Giotto came and in a moment the mystery was made plain, beam and heddles and treddles and reed fell into their proper places, and the old loom from the Flemings'-town, beside the Kent, unchanged in all important details from the loom that Florence at its noblest knew, was ready to weave into cloth whatever of thread the Langdale cottage dames would bring.

Coarseish thread and not without its knots and unevenness was the first that came from their old and rheumatic fingers, but the art was in their blood and the generations of those who had been mistresses of 'the divine spiral' had left an inheritance of aptitude, that in a surprisingly short time enabled them to spin thread fine enough for chalice veils and soft and delicate enough for a princess's apparel.

Not the least interesting part of the experiment was the social brightness brought into the lives of the villagers by the simple hospitalities of the Crag. Miss Twelves organised spinster tea-parties and the good old days of dale spinning-'does' once more returned. These were not allowed to degenerate into mere gossipings, for many a passage from the poets and from Ruskin was read aloud, and the aims of the Brantwood prophet and his good wishes to the adventure were spoken of.

If the renewed industry was fortunate in having as its originator a man who was an idealist and could by his facile pen make its prospects known to the public, it was as fortunate in having a practical woman and a most self-sacrificing and indefatigable enthusiast for Ruskin's teaching at its head to carry out all the difficult detail of starting the workers and organising the industrial effort. No words of mine are needed to put on record what the

Langdale Linen Industry owed in its first five years of uphill work to Miss Twelves. When she broke her connexion with that neighbourhood and came across the Raise gap to Keswick, she was able to know that she had not only established the fact that hand-spun linen could be produced at a price which the public, and specially the embroidering public, would pay for it, but she had seen enough of the pleasure brought into cottage homes by the humming wheel, to make her determined to do for Cumberland what she had done for Westmoreland, and by the help of a faithful spinner who followed her from Langdale, she set up her loom and her linen-boiler at St. Kentigern's, and within twelve months had organised a linen industry in connexion with our Keswick School of Industrial Arts. She broke this connexion after five years, and has since tackled the problem of linen-making quite independently, under the banner of good St. George in her quaint old cottage beside the Greta. Her good work has gone on uninterruptedly since. Just as at Langdale the embroiderer's art was added to advance the sale of the linen, so here at Keswick the embroideress has been encouraged and Miss Twelves has gathered round her,

workers of Sicilian and Greek embroidery,
who undertake the ornament of the linen spun
and woven.

But what had Ruskin to do with this work?
He had everything to do with it.   It was
the kindly message sent now and again of
heartfelt thanks to his tireless worker, it was
the handshake and the 'thank you, thank
you,' and the smile of his face whence the
faithlessness or lack of obedience of others
had driven the smile, that encouraged her as
it encouraged others to determine to carry out
the known wishes of the Master and to do
what in her was possible while health and
strength were hers to add to the mind's content
of her friend and teacher.   I have seen many
of these little messages sent to her through
Mrs. Severn, and I know how they were
appreciated.

The death hour came.   Her friend and her
inspirer to the task was borne from Brantwood
to the village church, and not the least solace
in those dark mournful hours was the thought
that at least the pall that lay upon the
Master's coffin was handspun and handwoven
here at Keswick under her own direction.
How far the work will be permanent here or
in Langdale cannot now be seen.   St. Martin's

THE KESWICK SCHOOL OF INDUSTRIAL ARTS.   From Photo. by Pettitt.

no longer enshrines the weavers by the banks of Elterwater, but on Holme ground, under the skilful hands of one of Miss Twelves' first pupils, the cloth is still made and silk has been added to the linen weft and warp. Nor would it be wise to prophesy that in the Keswick Vale women would 'swiftly turn the murmuring wheel' if Miss Twelves left us.

But at least it has been demonstrated that cottage hands can spin as deftly as of old, and love the task as their fore-elders loved it in the days gone by.—"You may take my life but you must not take my wheel," said a Langdale spinster to Mr. Fleming,—and it has been shown that the embroiderer's needle can have nothing more to be desired for ease in the working or for durability, and tender tone as background for the colour of the embroiderer's fancy than handspun and handwoven linen. As long as people read of Ruskin's life and influence, they will remember, as he has told us in the last letters he wrote to the members of his Guild of St. George, that the successful bringing back the old industry of the spinning wheel to the homes of Westmoreland was a subject of deepest interest to himself, and they will be grateful as he was grateful to those who brought it about.

K

Kindred to these two experiments in aim
and in inspiration was the work of Mr. and
Mrs. Alfred Harris, Kirkby Lonsdale, of
Mr. Alfred Willink at Burneside near Kendal.
Anyone who had the privilege, as I had on
more than one occasion, of seeing the youth
of Kirkby Lonsdale gathered together under
the teaching of Miss Harris at the drawing
school there, would have realised how truly
Ruskin's mind was over all. There in addition
to repoussé and wood-carving and leather work,
was added the interest of the potter's wheel.

Anyone who has ever visited Burneside
Church and delighted their eyes with the
carving of the reredos there would feel that
there too Ruskin's spirit had been at work,
the guardian and inspirer of village handicraft.

It is on the banks of Windermere to-day
that the visitor may find the latest and not
least sturdy plant of English handicraft of
wood-carving, spinning, and weaving in full
blossom. At Gill Head, Arthur Simpson, a
true follower of Ruskin's teaching, and one
who is proud of his profession as a maker and
designer of furniture for household purposes,
has been able to open a summer-school and
to help a good number of willing pupils each
year to learn something of the secrets of

wood-craft in such scenery as keeps the heart
at peace and the eyes filled with the reverence
for nature.

At Bowness, or to be accurate, at the
Spinney, Fairfield, just above the Crown Hotel,
Miss Garnett who was helped in her project
first by Mrs. Brownson and afterwards by Miss
Rawson, has been able to keep two experienced
weavers and assistants at work, and has got
round her quite an army of spinsters and
embroideresses. She teaches any villager to
spin without charge and has already found
employment for ninety hands. The days of
Exodus appeared to have returned. Here
as in the old Hebrew days, "All the women
who are wise-hearted do spin with their
hands and bring that which they have spun
both of blue and of purple and of scarlet and
of fine linen."

One of the varieties of textile fabric made is
a mixture of linen and silk called "Throwans,"
and old brocades are shortly to be made
upon the spinning loom. This weaving and
spinning and embroidery school cannot be
said to be directly connected with Brantwood,
but it was the direct resultant of the Langdale
linen experiment, and none the less does it
appear, as one talks with the promoter, that

here too is an example of the subtle way in which Ruskin's known wishes in the day of his health and hopefulness brought it about that in the day of his weakness and heart sadness, when he had retired from the world of action, there came to him cheer from loyal followers in the lakeland vales. Insignificant as these experiments in Home Art Industry were, the Master's desire for a happier England for the working man, seemed at last to find some promise of fulfilment. The Home Art Industries at the Lakes gave him true joy, and were welcomed by him with sincerest thankfulness and constant approval.

CHAPTER VI.

RUSKIN AND WORDSWORTH.

THOSE who remember John Ruskin's high estimate of Wordsworth's poetry in *Modern Painters*, and who compare it with his rather captious criticism of the poet in the papers entitled 'Fiction—Fair and Foul' which appeared in the *Nineteenth Century* of 1881, will wonder how this change in Ruskin's mind came about, and perhaps conclude a little hastily that Ruskin, beginning with enthusiasm for the Rydal poet's work, allowed that enthusiasm to cool off towards the end of his life.

It is not till we realise how much in common these two thinkers and workers at the English lakes had, in all their thought and work, that one understands that however as time went on there might be criticism, there was never any rift in the lute of their deep harmony, and that

as in death, so in life, and in their ideas of the
vital essentials of life, they cannot be divided.

Let us look first at *Modern Painters*. When
Ruskin sought for a prefatory poem for his first
great work, he turned to Wordsworth :

> "Accuse me not
> Of arrogance,
> If, having walked with Nature
> And offered, far as frailty would allow,
> My heart a daily sacrifice to Truth,
> I now affirm of Nature and of Truth
> Whom I have served, that their divinity
> Revolts offended at the ways of men."

In part ii., sec. i., chapter vii., of volume i.,
we find Ruskin contrasting the want of the
intense all-observing penetration of a well-
balanced mind amongst English landscapists,
with this quality in Wordsworth. " They have
not, " says he, " except in one or two instances,
anything of that feeling which Wordsworth
shews in the following lines :

> " 'So fair, so sweet, withal so sensitive;
> Would that the little flowers were born to live
> Conscious of half the pleasure which they give,
> That to this mountain daisy's self were known,
> *The beauty of its star-shaped shadow thrown*
> *On the smooth surface of this naked stone.'*

There is a bit of good downright foreground painting no mistake about it; drawing

and shadow and stone texture and all. Our
painters, " he adds, "must come to this before
they have done their duty."

In sec. ii., chapter iii., he again testifies
to the accurate observation of Wordsworth.
He is describing the shadows of the tree
trunks in Turner's drawing at page 163 of
Rogers' *Italy*, and he says, " Hear how
Wordsworth, the keenest-eyed of all modern
poets for what is deep and essential in nature,
illustrates Turner here, as we shall find him
doing at all other points :

> "' At the root
> Of that tall pine, the shadow of whose base
> And slender stem, while here I sat at eve,
> Oft stretches toward me like a long straight path
> Traced faintly in the greensward. '"

In sec. iii., chapter i., speaking of the
sky, he quotes Wordsworth again, " The sky
is for all—bright as it is, not

> "' Too bright nor good
> For human nature's daily food '"

and then, after criticising the conventional
way in which painters paint the heaven as if
it were a solid roof, a clear high material
dome, whose skies you may look at but
not through, Ruskin explains, that if there
be one characteristic of the sky more valuable

or necessary to be rendered than another, it is that which Wordsworth has given in the II. Book of 'The Excursion':

> "The dome of sky above my head
> Is Heaven's profoundest azure. No domain
> For fickle short-lived clouds to occupy
> Or to pass through—but rather an abyss
> In which the everlasting stars abide,
> And whose soft gloom and boundless depths might tempt
> The curious eye to look for them by day."

In the succeeding chapters, after shewing how in ancient landscape there was little or no attempt to paint the upper cloud region, Ruskin again appeals to the "fine and faithful" descriptive passage of 'The Excursion,' already alluded to, and shews how accurately and with what consummate carefulness, Wordsworth's infallible eye had described in the "crown of the blue firmament," the "multitudes of little floating clouds" vivid as fire.

If we take the second volume of *Modern Painters* in hand, we find in sec. i., chapter vii., that Ruskin, writing of Repose, and the figures under which men express their ideas of it, must needs go to Wordsworth, and as an example quote from the leech-gatherer his lines about the cloud,

> "That heareth not the loud winds when they call
> And moveth all together, if it move at all."

In sec. i., chapter xii., Ruskin, speaking
of the Theoretic Faculty, tells us that its "first
perfection relating to vital beauty is the kindness and unselfish fulness of heart which receives the utmost amount of pleasure from the
happiness of all things." He quotes Wordsworth's well-known lines in 'Hartleap Well'
and 'The White Doe of Rylstone' to shew
our duty of tenderest regard for animals.

Then he proceeds to speak of the way in
which, by sympathy, men can feel for inani-
mate nature, for flowers as well as animals.
"I would fain hold, if I might, 'the faith
that every flower enjoys the air it breathes!'"

"The sympathy of very sensitive minds
usually reaches so far as to the conception of
life in the plant, and so to love as with
Shakespeare always, as he has taught us in
the sweet voices of Ophelia and Perdita, and
Wordsworth always, as of the daffodils and
the celandine—

> "'It doth not love the shower nor seek the cold;
> This neither is its courage nor its choice
> But its necessity in being old'—

and so all other great poets."

It is, I think, a fair inference to say that
when Ruskin wrote that last passage he was
thinking of Wordsworth as among the poets

of the first rank, for after the words "and so
all other great poets," he bids us in a footnote compare Milton's words about the
flowers :

> "They at her coming sprang
> And touched by her fair tendance gladlier grew."

When Ruskin penned that footnote, he
was much more of Matthew Arnold's mind in
his estimate of Wordsworth's place among the
immortals than he seems to have been at a
later day. "Dante, Shakespeare, Molière,
Milton, Goethe are altogether larger and more
splendid luminaries in the poetical heavens
than Wordsworth," said Matthew Arnold,
"but I know not where else among the
moderns we are to find his superiors. He is
one of the very chief glories of English
poetry, and by nothing is England so glorious
as by her poetry."

I have quoted these words from Matthew
Arnold's preface to his *Selections from
Wordsworth's Poems* because Ruskin alludes
to the book in the trenchant criticism that
seems to belittle Wordsworth in the second
chapter of 'Fiction—Fair and Foul.' Ruskin
had just seen *The Selections*, and read 'with
sincerest interest Matthew Arnold's estimate
of the poems,' but he begs us to remember

that "Wordsworth's rank and scale among
the poets were determined by himself in a
single exclamation :

"'What was the great Parnassus' self to thee,
Mount Skiddaw ? '

Answer this question faithfully and you have
the relation between the great masters of
the Muse's teaching and the pleasant fingerer
of the pastoral flute among the reeds of
Rydal," and then he proceeds to do his best
to pull down the Wordsworthian idol and lay
the Rydalian laurels in the dust, and not
quite in the kindest way, either. Doubtless
there is much truth in the criticism, but there
is a depreciative undertone that outlasts the
kindlier notes of real appreciation with which
the chapter concludes :

"Wordsworth is simply a Westmoreland
peasant, with considerably less shrewdness
than most border Englishmen or Scotsmen
inherit ; and no sense of humour : but gifted
(in this singularly) with vivid sense of natural
beauty, and a pretty turn for reflections, not
always acute, but, as far as they reach,
medicinal to the fever of the restless and
corrupted life around him. Water to parched
lips may be better than Samian wine, but do
not let us therefore confuse the qualities of

wine and water. I much doubt there being many inglorious Miltons in our country church-yards; but I am very sure there are many Wordsworths resting there, who were inferior to the renowned one only in caring less to hear themselves talk.

"With an honest and kindly heart, a stimu-lating egoism, a wholesome contentment in modest circumstances, and such sufficient ease, in that accepted state, as permitted the passing of a good deal of time in wishing that daisies could see the beauty of their own shadows, and other such profitable mental exercises, Wordsworth has left us a series of studies of the graceful and happy shepherd life of our lake country, which to me person-ally, for one, are entirely sweet and precious; but they are only so as the mirror of an existent reality in many ways more beautiful than its picture.

" But the other day I went for an afternoon's rest into the cottage of one of our country people of old statesman class; cottage lying nearly midway between two village churches, but more conveniently for downhill walk to-wards one than the other. I found, as the good housewife made tea for me, that never-theless she went up the hill to church. 'Why

do not you go to the nearer church?' I
asked. 'Don't you like the clergyman?'
'Oh no, sir,' she answered, 'it isn't that;
but you know I couldn't leave my mother.'
'Your mother! she is buried at H——, then?'
'Yes sir; and you know I couldn't go to
church anywhere else.'

"That feelings such as these existed among
the peasants, not of Cumberland only, but of all
the tender earth that gives forth her fruit for
the living, and receives her dead to peace,
might perhaps have been, to our great and
endless comfort, discovered before now, if
Wordsworth had been content to tell us what
he knew of his own villages and people, not
as the leader of a new and only correct
school of poetry, but simply as a country
gentleman of sense and feeling, fond of prim-
roses, kind to the parish children, and rever-
ent of the spade with which Wilkinson had
tilled his lands; and I am by no means sure
that his influence on the stronger minds of
his time was anywise hastened or extended
by the spirit of tunefulness under whose
guidance he discovered that heaven rhymed
to seven, and Foy to boy.

"Tuneful nevertheless at heart, and of the
heavenly choir, I gladly and frankly acknow-

ledge him; and our English literature enriched
with a new and a singular virtue in the aerial
purity and healthful rightness of his quiet
song;—but *aerial* only,—not ethereal; and
lowly in its privacy of light.

"A measured mind, and calm; innocent,
unrepentant; helpful to sinless creatures and
scathless, such of the flock as do not stray.
Hopeful at least, if not faithful; content with
intimations of immortality such as may be in
skipping of lambs, and laughter of children—
incurious to see in the hands the print of the
Nails.

"A gracious and constant mind; as the
herbage of its native hills, fragrant and pure;
—yet, to the sweep and the shadow, the
stress and distress, of the greater souls of
men, as the tufted thyme to the laurel wilderness of Tempe,—as the gleaming euphrasy to
the dark branches of Dodona."

It is fair to suggest if one takes the fourth
chapter of 'Fiction—Fair and Foul' in hand,
that Ruskin's bile had been moved not so
much against the poet as against his school
of followers, the 'amiable Wordsworthians' of
his day.

He knew how few of those who professed
a love of Wordsworth had an intimate ac-

quaintance with the poet's work. He knew
how comparatively small a number of the
professors ever put in practice a single
syllable of the advice tendered them by their
model poet, and smarting, as he did smart
from the same misfortune of having abundant
disciples in word and not in deed, he visited
his vials of indignation upon these amiable
Wordsworthians by dethroning their king, or
attempting to shew that their opinion of his
highness was sentimental and not founded on
a true critical estimate.

" I happen myself," he says, "to have used
Wordsworth as a daily text-book from youth
to age, and have lived moreover in all
essential points according to the tenor of his
teaching."—Could praise go further? He
adds, " I know more vitally than my bucolic
friends what is in Wordsworth and what is
not. Any man who chooses to live by his
precepts will thankfully find in them a beauty
and rightness (*exquisite* rightness I called it
in *Sesame and Lilies*) which will preserve
him alike from mean pleasure, vain hope and
guilty deed. . . So that he will neither moan
at the gate of the fields which with covetous
spirit he sold, nor drink of the waters which
with yet more covetous spirit he stole, nor

devour the bread of the poor in secret, nor set on his guest-table the poor man's lamb. In all these homely virtues and assured justices let him be Wordsworth's true disciple and he will be able with equanimity to hear it said when there is need to say so, that his excellent master often wrote verses that were not musical and sometimes expressed opinions that were not profound."

Ruskin then proceeds at rather unnecessary length to criticise the want of music and the lack of real understanding of the facts of history in the thirty-eighth ecclesiastical sonnet,

"Amazement strikes the crowd : while many turn,"

and after an elaborate history of the facts that led up to the Truce of Venice, and the Peace of Constance, he begs his reader "with the clues now given,"—whatever he may ultimately feel or affirm as to the Devil's part in the Venetian Truce or Constantian Peace. "This at least he will please note for positive, that Mr. Wordsworth having no shadow of doubt of the complete wisdom of any idea that comes into his own head, writes down in dogmatic sonnet his first impression of black instrumentality in the business," to the deluding of his innocent readers.

Doubtless Wordsworth was dogmatic and did believe his thoughts on most subjects were as he once expressed it to a friend, 'very valooable.' Doubtless he sometimes expressed himself as though he had the whole truth and nothing but the truth. But it is open to question, whether it is not this very likeness in the two men, this similar leaning to dogmatic utterance, this same pleasure in hearing themselves give utterance to all the thoughts of their hearts, that made it almost certain that each would have a certain mistrust of the other. That really seems to be the explanation of some of the more caustic criticism and little ill-natured pokings of fun at his master and mentor which Ruskin sometimes indulged in.

There was of course a great gulf between them in knowledge of Art history and Art criticism. The colour sense that made it impossible for Ruskin to care for the coarse yellow of the celandine was probably not developed in the older poet. The manners of the men were very different. The absolute naturalness and swift and eager enthusiasms, the entire absence of self-satisfaction or self-esteem in the one, would be certain to feel critical of the colder manner of the other

L

which sometimes seemed to verge upon pomposity; but if we will take the trouble to read again Ruskin's belief in the beauty and rightness of Wordsworth's words, and in 'the homely virtues and assured justices' that Wordsworth taught, we shall find that Ruskin, who more than most men of his day had a right to criticise literary work, and a heart to understand the gospel which Wordsworth and he both taught, was able to feel the truth of Wordsworth's own estimate of his powers. "They will co-operate with the benign tenderness in human nature and society and will in their degree be efficacious in making men wiser, better, and happier."

CHAPTER VII.

RUSKIN AND WORDSWORTH.

(Continued.)

IT was unfortunate for Ruskin's early education in the love and study of the poets that his father was not a Wordsworthian.

The home-bred boy who was scrupulously taught his Bible and Latin grammar by his mother, was as fondly and devotedly taught his Scott and his Pope and his Byron by his father. But anyone who will read of Ruskin's early intuition of Nature's power to "kindle or restrain," or of that marvellous, overwhelming power to impress, to captivate and fill the heart with its own overflowing joy, which he tells us he felt last at the age of eighteen, must perceive that there was a wondrous common sympathy in the minds of these two Nature lovers, and that they saw more nearly with a common eye than Ruskin latterly supposed.

For what after all was Wordsworth's gift to
his time than that he perceived beneath the
outward form of natural beauty,

> " A motion and a spirit that impels
> All thinking things, all objects of all thought,
> And rolls through all things."

It was just this vision of the deeply spiritual
side of things seen which made Ruskin from
his boyhood so determined an exponent of the
spirit, and so earnest in his combat with
materialism.

When Mr. Holman Hunt, at the unveiling of
the Ruskin Memorial tablet in the Church
of St. Paul at Herne Hill, on the first birthday
after Ruskin's death, wished to point to the
essential work in the world of letters and art
that Ruskin achieved, he could but say that he
had imported into literature that was frivolous,
a serious earnestness, and into art a high
purpose.   Ruskin found that art was purpose-
less ; he found that the pendulum of art had
swayed in the direction of materialism, and he
wanted it to turn in the direction of spiritualism.

Of what two men in the Victorian era can it
be more truly said that they were filled with a
divine earnestness to solve the question of how
to live rightly, than of these two poets of the
English Lakes, Wordsworth and Ruskin ; for

Ruskin's prose is poetry.   Great in their noble
and profound application of ideas to common
life; at heart reformers, the text of their
discoursing was identical, 'on Man on Nature
and on Human Life.'   They sang of or wrote
of the same great realities :

> "Of truth, of goodness, beauty, love and hope
> And melancholy fear subdued by death,
> Of blessed consolations in distress,
> Of moral strength and intellectual power,
> Of joy in widest commonalty spread."

They believed one gospel,

> "We live by admiration, hope and love."

They cared for the simplicities of life with the
same care.   They hated Mammon-worship with
the same hate, and though one was more
independent of blame or praise than the other,
they each had the same dogmatic and dictatorial
intuitions that truth as they saw it was the whole
truth.   Each had the same love of the country
and horror of the town.   Each heard the same
'human wailing' in our wildernesses of brick
and mortar, the cry

> "Of sorrow barricadoed evermore
> Within the walls of cities."

And each found in Nature more than in Man
the calm that strengthens and the sympathy
that makes companionship.

Yet this very sameness of aim in work and likeness of disposition seems to have set them apart. It may be true that Ruskin's father did not in early days take steps to cast the spell of Wordsworth about his growing boy; it may be true that the boy's first impressions of Wordsworth when, on his famous Iteriad journey, he saw him in the Grasmere Church, were not in favour of the Rydal bard, but it is quite clear that, unknowing of Wordsworth's canons of taste, young Ruskin as an undergraduate saw with the same eyes and thought with the same thought on Man and Nature.

It is quite remarkable to note how Ruskin's early thoughts about the right building of Westmoreland cottages, and the peculiar beauty of their fitness to their surroundings, are but echoes of Wordsworth's observation and dicta as laid down in his *Guide-book to the Lakes*.

That wondrous power upon the soul that a beautiful scene has with Wordsworth was certainly as strong with young Ruskin; and both felt its dwindling power as years brought on their power to blunt the mind. There were times when as Wordsworth tells us,

"like a roe
He bounded o'er the mountains by the sides

Of the deep rivers and the lonely streams
Wherever Nature led."

In those times he writes,

"The sounding cataract
Haunted me like a passion, the tall rock
The mountain and the deep and gloomy wood
Their colours and their forms were then to me
An appetite : a feeling and a love."

No one who remembers how Ruskin spoke of his young days when the rivers led him on, and the blue hills filled his dreams, but must feel how both these men, from Nature and her overflowing soul received so much that all their thoughts were steeped in feeling. And as one gradually follows the growth of their minds, one sees the same fading of her first power to impress ; Wordsworth's own experience,

"There was a time when meadow, grove, and stream,
The earth, and every common sight,
To me did seem
Apparelled in celestial light,
The glory and the freshness of a dream.
It is not now as it hath been of yore ;—
Turn wheresoe'er I may
By night or day,
The things which I have seen I now can see no more.

One of the saddest talks I ever had with Ruskin was a talk about this transient power of the beauty of natural scenes to captivate and

hold the mind so soon as it hears beneath the
the veil of its loveliness

> "The still sad music of humanity."

But to the end of life, Wordsworth's experience was Ruskin's experience also, and each
to the last hour of their working-day could truly
have said,

> "I have felt
> A presence that disturbs me with the joy
> Of elevated things : a sense sublime
> Of something far more deeply interfused
> Whose dwelling is the light of setting suns.
> And the round ocean and the living air
> And the blue sky and in the mind of man
> Therefore am I still
> A lover of the meadows and the woods,
> And mountains ; and of all the mighty world
> Of eye, and ear,—both what they half create,
> And what perceive ; well pleased to recognise
> In nature and the language of the sense,
> The anchor of my purest thoughts, the nurse,
> The guide, the guardian of my heart, and soul
> Of all my moral being."

They had the same thoughts about the need
of keeping inviolate the sanctuary for thought
and health and national happiness which the
English Lake District, still undestroyed and
unvulgarised, truly is.

Read Wordsworth's protest against the projected railway from Kendal to Windermere,

and set side by side with it Ruskin's preface
to the pamphlet entitled *A Protest against
the Extension of Railways in the Lake
District.* The feeling and the spirit of both
writers are the same. They had the same
reverential regard for the life of the simple
dalesmen amongst whom they dwelt. There
are few tenderèr pictures of cottage life than
Wordsworth's description of Margaret and
Michael. You will find that Ruskin, who
spoke of the men about his door as knights
at Agincourt whose words for a thousand
pounds was their bond, did but echo the
feeling for Westmoreland peasantry that
Wordsworth gave utterance to.

It may be true that Ruskin stood in nearer
relation to the peasants than the poet.
Wordsworth, as the tradition in the dales still
goes, "was not a vara conversable man at
best o' times," and when he speaks of Michael
he classes him with

> "Shepherds, dwellers in the valleys, men
> Whom I already loved ;—*not verily
> For their own sakes* but for the fields and hills
> Where was their occupation and abode ";

whereas with Ruskin, what he seemed most
to care about was to go to the cottage or to
the workshop, and be made by his tender

approachableness one of the family. But both believed in the true-hearted, innate nobility of the dalesmen, and honoured them for their native worth.

The poet who in so much that he wrote glorified the peasant's lot by shewing the peasant could think high thoughts as he pursued his lowly calling, and prove himself a happy warrior as he wrestled with storm and heat and all the sorrow of a poor man's lot, was after all but expressing the mind of Ruskin. Nay was himself an embodiment of Ruskin's ideal, as all who visit Dove Cottage to-day may testify.

" In order to teach men how to be satisfied it is necessary fully to understand the art and joy of humble life . . . the life of domestic affection and domestic peace, and full of sensitiveness to all elements of costless and kind pleasure, therefore chiefly to the loveliness of the natural world " so wrote Ruskin.

It was surely to teach this lesson of blessed content that Wordsworth lived and sang.

" It is not," says Ruskin, " that men are ill-fed, but they have no pleasure in their work by which they make their bread, and therefore look to wealth as the only means of pleasure."

This Wordsworth knew, and whether he
was sketching the picture of the priest of the
Duddon Valley, or "Wonderful Walker" at
Seathwaite, or the firm-minded Leech-gatherer,
or the cheerful-hearted School-master, he seems
to have felt and told us that the quiet mind
that labours and is content, has found
enough of the will of God for men on
earth to make the journey to the end a way
of peace, Of no two writers in our Victorian
age can it be more truly said that they
agreed in their belief that a nation's wealth
was not mammon but men, and that labour in
the country side had peculiar dignity and
calm, and might have therewithal content.

It was not only the peasant, but the
peasant's children that were dear to Wordsworth and to Ruskin. Go into any cottage
in Coniston to-day and hear how it is the
pride of the cottage to remember that when
Janie or Ellen or Agnes went to school, Mr.
Ruskin never passed them without a word.
It is true that this could not be said of
Wordsworth, " They were flayte to deeath of
him wi' his girt voice and his ' bummin' along
t'rwoad"; but none who have read Wordsworth's tenderest poem, " Lucy Gray," We Are
Seven," " The Pet Lamb," " Three Years She

Grew in Sun and Shower," "She Dwelt Among
the Untrodden Ways";—none who remember
Wordsworth's grief when his own children,
little Catherine and Thomas, were taken from
him, but must feel that the child life and the
child mind was very dear to him, and that
of many children in the dales beside Barbara
Lewthwaite it might be truly said by Wordsworth and Ruskin alike

"She looked with such a look and she spoke with such a tone
That I almost received her heart into my own."

The bairns are fair to see. Go where you
will in the dales, the healthy, happy looks, the
fine complexions and the bright eyes, the
regular features of the children of the old
Viking stock are very noticeable, and there is
a delicacy of manner, a natural lady-likeness
about the girls, and a precocious manliness
about the boys and a naturalness about both
that is very taking. Ruskin and Wordsworth
seemed to share the belief in the educative
power of scenery. Both knew how scenery
and the love of it could stir

"The passions that build up the human soul
Not with the mean and vulgar works of men
But with high objects with enduring things,"

And it is worth while remembering that if
for Wordsworth it is true that as a boy in

the Esthwaite and Hawkshead valley, "fair
seed-time had his soul," the heart of Ruskin
as a lad was touched by the beauty of the
same Furness fells, and Raven Crag and
Wetherlam and Tarn Hause, that had so much
to do with the moulding of Wordsworth's
mind ; and both might have written of Westmoreland and Cumberland scenery : that it

"While I was yet a boy
Careless of books, yet having felt the power
Of Nature by the gentle agency
Of Natural objects, led me on to feel
For passions that were not my own and think
On man the heart of man and human life."

But it is specially as to the power of
scenery to educate the mind insensibly that
Ruskin and Wordsworth seem in such close
agreement. Wordsworth writes :

"grossly that man errs, who should suppose
That the green valleys and the streams and rocks
Were things indifferent to the Shepherd's thoughts.
. . . .
Those fields, those hills—what could they less—had laid
Strong hold on his affections, were to him
A pleasureable feeling of blind love,
The pleasure which there is in life itself."

Now let us turn from 'Michael' to 'The
Brothers' and picture to ourselves how Leonard
the shepherd as Wordsworth drew him heard

" in the piping shrouds the tones of waterfalls,"
and among the broad blue waves and spark-
ling foam, saw the forms of sheep that grazed
on verdant hills, and felt himself again in
Cumberland. The quiet power of the scenery
to impress, even if it was not much talked
about, was known to both.

> "Love had he found in huts where poor men lie
> His daily teachers had been woods and hills
> The silence that is in the starry sky
> The sleep that is among the lonely hills,"

This was true of Wordsworth and of Ruskin
as it was of the Shepherd Lord. Both taught
us, for both had experience, how

> " To her fair works did Nature link,
> The human soul that through him ran,"

and how this linking of the calm and peace
and kindliness and joy and generosity of
natural beauty trains, strengthens, educates
and rebukes the heart.

" There are few," writes Ruskin, "who do
not receive, and do not know that they receive at certain moments, strength of some
kind or rebuke from the appealings of outward things. And it is not possible for a
Christian man to walk across so much as a
rood of the natural earth with mind unagitated
and rightly poised, without receiving strength

and hope from some stone, flower, leaf or sound; nor without a sense of a dew falling upon him out of the sky."

And from both Wordsworth and Ruskin comes the same message to our hot and eager time, that in patience we should possess our souls and trust more than is our wont to this great kindly Nature to feed and to sustain, and learn to cultivate the power to commune with her and be still.

> " The eye—it cannot choose but see
> We cannot bid the ear be still ;
> Our bodies feel, where'er they be,
> Against or with our will.
>
> Nor less I deem that there are Powers
> Which of themselves our minds impress ;
> That we can feed this mind of ours
> In a wise passiveness.
>
> Think you, 'mid all this mighty sum
> Of things for ever speaking,
> That nothing of itself will come,
> But we must still be seeking ! "

As we read these stanzas from Wordsworth's "Expostulation and Reply" do we not understand why it was that Ruskin pleaded for "that majestic indolence so dear to native men," which Wordsworth taught when he urged the quiet unconscious receiving of impressions from Nature. Do we not

hear Ruskin's voice saying, " I tell you truly
that to a quiet heart and healthy brain and
industrous hand there is more delight and
use in the dappling of one wood glade with
flowers and sunshine, than to the restless,
heartless and idle could be brought by a
panorama of and belt of the world photo-
graphed round the equator. " But

> " The eye—it cannot choose but see
> We cannot bid the ear be still
> Our bodies feel, where'er they be,
> Against or with our will."

It was because of this that Wordsworth
and Ruskin strove to keep our twenty miles
square of inspiring and inspiriting scenery
' secure from rash assault.' It was in the
mountains they had felt the weight of their
desire. They knew how these Westmoreland
and Cumberland fells could impress men's
souls with their "wise pensiveness." And it
was because the eye cannot ' choose but see'
that Ruskin pleaded in Wordsworthian spirit
for the educative power of beautiful surroundings. " To cultivate sympathy you must be
among living creatures, and thinking about
them." " All education to beauty," writes
Ruskin, "is first in beauty of gentle faces
round a child, secondly in the fields."

But Ruskin and Wordsworth also knew that men lost the power to be impressed if they are always in the presence of the marvellous beauty of mountain and of vale. "Custom," sang Wordsworth,

> "Custom hangs upon us with a weight
> Heavy as frost and deep almost as life."

And Ruskin has told us that he "believed that what Wordsworth spoke of as a glory in the child because it had come fresh from God's hands, was in reality nothing more than the freshness of all things to its newly opened sight. "I find," says he, "that by keeping long away from the hills, I can in great part still restore the old childish feeling about them, and the more I live and work among them, the more it vanishes."

There is probably no better passage in Ruskin's work to shew how he saw eye to eye with Wordsworth in the matter of the educative power of natural scenery and the country life, than the passage in the second chapter of *Sesame and Lilies* entitled 'Queens' Gardens,' wherein, speaking of duties to a young girl in training her to perfect womanhood, he quotes Wordsworth's poem, "Three Years She Grew in Sun and Shower," and specially asks his readers to notice the last of the four stanzas :

M

"And vital feelings of delight
    Shall rear her form to stately height,
    Her virgin bosom swell;
    Such thoughts to Lucy I will give
    While she and I together live
    Here in this happy dell."

He emphasises the need of the naturalness
of the process of education, and the joy of it.
Ruskin held that the end of education was to
make a child of Nature and a human being.
He seems to suggest, as he quotes the poem,
how necessary to the vital influences of education, is the free spontaneous gift of natural
sound and scene to the growing girl: how
needful it was that she should as spontaneously
receive the boon and blessedness of Nature's
beauty; and Wordsworth, of whom in this connection Ruskin bears witness that he is a poet
distinguished from all others not by power,
but 'by exquisite rightness,' laid our country-
men, or so many of them as rightly care for
right education, under constant obligation, by
his assertion of the same truth that Ruskin
taught.

It has been before said that Ruskin and
Wordsworth saw eye to eye in the prime need
of our national education, which has to turn
out men, not machines; men, not money. Let
anyone read *Unto This Last* and then take

such a sonnet in hand as that written in October of 1803. "These times touch monied worldlings with dismay," and see how truly the poet contrasted the paralysis of a nation—

"When men change swords for ledgers, and desert
The student's banner for gold "—

with that undying hopefulness that comes of contented toil in the open air, whose joy it is to 'draw hard breath above the plough-share,'

"Sound healthy children of the God of Heaven
As cheerful as the rising sun in May."

The gospel that Wordsworth brought to the healing of his time, the beginning of the nineteenth century :

"That virtue and the faculties within
Are vital — and that riches are akin
To years, to change, to cowardice and death ! "

was the same gospel that Ruskin with clarion tone proclaimed as the salvation of the ending of the same century. Each felt that the curse of their time was greed of gain.

"The world is too much with us; late and soon,
Getting and spending, we lay waste our powers
Little we see in Nature that is ours,
We have given our hearts away a sordid boon ! "

Each felt that

> "The heroic wealth of hall and bower
> Had forfeited their ancient English dower
> Of inward happiness."

And you may almost hear Ruskin's voice of passionate sorrow, tender in its pity and heart, appealing in its earnestness of lament, saying, in Wordsworth's verse:

> "O Friend! I know not which way I must look
> For comfort, being as I am opprest,
> To think that now our life is only drest
> For show: mean handywork of craftsman, cook,
> Or groom. We must run glittering like a brook,
> In the open sunshine or we are unblest:
> The wealthiest man among us is the best;
> No grandeur now in nature or in book
> Delights us. Rapine, avarice, expense,
> This is idolatry and these we adore;
> Plain living and high thinking are no more:
> The homely beauty of the good old cause
> Is gone; Our peace, our fearful innocence
> And pure religion, healthy household laws."

But though these seers sorrowed, they both sorrowed not as without hope, and the poet who felt that

> "altar, sword and pen,
> Fire-side—the heroic wealth of hall and bower,
> Have forfeited their ancient English dower
> Of inward happiness"

knew also that

> "in our halls was hung
> Armoury of the invincible knights of old."

Felt also that

> "in every thing we are sprung
> Of earth's best blood, have titles manifold,"

and Ruskin knew this and felt this. His founding of the Guild of St. George was but a recall to ancient knightliness, and when he got some of the young undergraduates at Oxford to take the spade and mend the broken way for the Hinksey villagers, he did it in the spirit of cheeriest optimism, and told the men he taught that he thought England would yet learn wherein true nobility consisted, and recognise the helpers of the people as their knights royal, their very perfect gentlemen. In nothing more did Ruskin seem to feel knightliness consisted than in the power to be pitiful and just. And he who wrote as the 4th Rule in the creed for the members of St. George's Guild,—"I will not deceive or cause to be deceived any human being for my gain or pleasure, nor hurt, or cause to be hurt any human being for my gain or pleasure," wrote also in the Rule following, "I will not kill nor hurt any living creature needlessly nor destroy any beautiful thing, but will strive to save and comfort all gentle life and guard and perfect all natural beauty upon earth."

It was in the same spirit that Wordsworth wrote that last stanza in Hartleap Well,

> "One lesson, Shepherd, let us two divide
> Taught both by what she shows, and what conceals
> Never to blend our pleasure or our pride
> With sorrow of the meanest thing that feels,"

and bade us to know that he

> "Who cannot feel for every living thing
> Hath faculties that he hath never used."

That tender regard too which Ruskin always felt for tree and plant and moss was felt by Wordsworth. An old Rydal Mount servant once said to me, "Mr. Wudsworth could not abear to see so much as a stean, nor a flower moved." What he said was borne out by the inscription for a stone in the grounds of Rydal Mount. Doubtless both men felt that God had lent us this beautiful earth of ours, and that it was, as Ruskin put it, 'a great entail' only for our life, that it belonged as much to those who are to come after us, that in consequence we had no right by anything we did or neglected to do 'to deprive them of benefits which it was in our power to bequeath.'

But as with bird life, so with flower life. Though Wordsworth loved the daisy and the lesser celandine and the daffodil and the wild geranium, and Ruskin cared most for the wilding rose, they both felt these gentle things a kind of sacred presence in field and hedgerow, and I never can think of Wordsworth singing,

"The chosen plants and blossoms blown
Among the distant mountains, flower and weed,"

to that "orchard garden eminently fair," at Town End, Grasmere; I can never think of his building the rockery round the little spring in Dove Cottage garden, without the thought of the loving way in which Ruskin would point out the wild flowers he had transplanted from the fell to bloom near his woodland streamlet at Brantwood, without remembrance of his tender regard for all flower life he ever passed in field or moor. Each saw with an inevitable eye and noted the ways of flowers and birds and animals as any lover could do. Each felt the varying changes of the year. How often does the line, "It is the first glad day of March," ring up in Ruskin's letters. Compare the inimitable description of a squirrel's ways as given in the lecture delivered at Kendal with the delightful picture Wordsworth paints for us of the green linnet in the hazel tree—that 'brother of the dancing leaves,' that the poet spoke of as, "thyself thy own enjoyment."

In early days it was assuredly this truth to nature in his power of observation that attracted Ruskin to Wordsworth, as is clear from the passage quoted at the beginning of this chapter from *Modern Painters*, part ii., chapter iii., about the keen sight of Wordsworth for what was deep and essential in nature.

It is certain that if men are to be judged of as being kindred in soul by their common love of a friend, Ruskin and Wordsworth in their enthusiasm for Sir Walter Scott may be said to have had one heart, and both were curiously dependent upon woman's help and woman's friendship. It is true that the poet had a daughter and that Ruskin had none, but what Dora was to Wordsworth as a maker of home until she married, Mrs. Severn was to Ruskin; and those who read *Hortus Inclusus* will see that what Dorothy was to the Rydal bard, in encouragement, admiration and suggestion, so in a real way was Miss Susy Beever to the poet at Brantwood.

But it was not the common admiration of friends, or common need for the encouragement that friends could give, that made Wordsworth and Ruskin kin. It was rather their common

perception of vital truth.   If ever two minds
could walk together because they were agreed,
it was in the assertion that men could only truly
live their highest and happiest spirit life here on
earth in communion with Nature, if first they
could perceive that Nature was a revelation of
God's spirit and then could wonder and love
it with deepest reverence.   " The Spirit of
God," so wrote Ruskin, " is around you, in the
air that you breathe.   His glory in the light
that you see, and in the fruitfulness of the earth
and the joy of its creature.   He has written for
you day by day, His revelation as He has
granted you day by day your daily bread."
And again, " All this passing to and fro of
fruitful shower and grateful shade, and all these
visions of silver palaces built above the horizon,
and of moaning winds and waters, and glories of
coloured cloud and cloven ray, really are but to
deepen in our hearts the acceptance and
distinctness and clearness of the simple words,
' Our Father which art in Heaven.' "

The poet who wrote *Devotional Incitements*,
and who felt that glorious scene from Holm-
ground or Oxenfell so moved him when,

" Magnificent
The morning rose in memorable pomp,"

felt also that all this beauty, all this " sweetness

of a common dawn" was but a call to him
to vow his life to God. It was communing
with God or Nature that Wordsworth found
removed him " from little animosities and low
desires." It was 'towards the Uncreated' that
with transport of great joy he looked 'with
every form of creature' as he communed. For
Wordsworth more than anyone, Ruskin ex-
cepted, in our century,

> "Felt the sentiment of being spread
> O'er all that moves and all that seemeth still
> O'er all that lost beyond the reach of thought
> And human knowledge, to the human eye
> Invisible, yet liveth to the heart."

But only in deep reverence could such
communing be. "We live by Admiration,
Hope and Love," to this assertion Ruskin said
with full heart Amen. " As a child," he writes,
" I had in my little clay pitcher vialfulls as
it were of Wordsworth's reverence." And
speaking of this great central doctrine of
Wordsworth he tells us in *Fors* :—" Admiration,
Hope and Love. Three unmaterial things,
essential to life. No one knows how to live till
he has got them." And again, " I take Wordsworth's single line for my literal guide in all
education." In his Lecture on Art, Ruskin
amplifies his explanation of the word, "Admira-

tion."   "This is the thing which I know—that in Reverence is the chief joy and power of life. Reverence for what is pure and bright in your own youth ; for what is true and tried in the age of others : for all that is gracious among the living, great among the dead and marvellous in the powers that cannot die."

With this evangel of the vital needs of Admiration, Hope and Love, these two prophets of the Lord, helped their generation. Fallen asleep—the one in 1850, the other in 1900, all that is mortal of them rest in lakeland earth.   Grasmere Churchyard and Coniston Churchyard are now individually consecrated ; and pilgrims to either shrine will think of the double debt we owe, and hear not one but two clarion voices calling us, to lowlier reverence, loftier hopes, and love for men and Nature more devout.

They will hear within the voices of these seers a word of warning.   This little twenty mile square of hill and dale fed their souls with noblest passion, and lifted up their hearts to noblest heights.   Every year the quiet and the seclusion of it is threatened, every year its unspoiled beauty is in jeopardy.   No one who truly cares for the future of Great Britain, can think of this National Resting-ground

robbed of its healing charm,—its power to
inspire and invigorate the thought of the
present, or illustrate and enforce the thought of
the past.   All that is mortal of Wordsworth
rests in Grasmere Churchyard; all that is
mortal of Ruskin lies at Coniston.   But we are
false to the trust that they gave the tender
earth of the countryside they loved so truly
if we will not listen to their spirit words,
and strive as well as we may to keep the
land of their inspiration a heritage for the
helpful thought, the highest pleasure, and the
fullest peace of the generations yet to be.

CHAPTER VIII.

AT RUSKIN'S FUNERAL.

WE had been expecting his release from the frail 'body of this death' any time in the past three or four years. The Master whose fire and fervour and restless energy of brain and tireless hand had done the work of three men for St. George and Merrie England, had been all this while sitting at Brantwood, as it were, with folded hands, waiting, with calm serenity, for his angel friend. And very kindly and with tenderness of approach had Death at last come.

A little touch of feverish cold, a retiring to his bed for a single day, and then a sinking into that "golden slumber" spoken of in the song whose music last fell upon his willing ears; and then his eyes, with their memory of St. Gothard as Turner saw it, still undimmed, closed, and he went beyond the pass that is

so cold, and sometimes so full of storm and
pain, into the land of life and peace and endless
spring.

Almost it would seem as if the heavens built
their gates of gold and opened doors of glory
for his bright spirit's welcoming. The day had
been a day of cloud and storm. The hills,
purple black, had stood in gloom above a
leaden lake, when, on Friday, January 19, 1900,
the call came. Ruskin sank to rest, and sudden
radiance seemed showered out of heaven. A
great light lay upon the water-flood, cloud-
bastions of fire reared themselves above the
hills, and such splendour fell on Coniston and
Wetherlam and the russet crags of Tilberthwaite and Yewdale that the shepherd stared
and the yeoman wondered, and the mourners
took it for a sign. On Saturday, the 20th of
January, within a few weeks of fulfilling the
eighty-first year—for John Ruskin was born
on the 8th of February, 1819—the laborious
life of art criticism, of thought for the helping
of the world, of high ideals, of noble philosophy,
of impassioned utterance, of continual benevolence, was laid down without a sigh.

The funeral was fixed for the following
Thursday. Westminster opened its portals to
receive him, but Mrs. Arthur Severn was firm;

she knew her cousin's wish, and she respected
it. Writing to me after the funeral, she said :
" I knew he deserved to rest in the Abbey, but
my conscience does not reproach me for letting
him rest in the shadow of the mountains he
daily delighted to look upon ; and he hated
towns ! "

Those who gazed upon him in his last sleep
spoke of the gentleness of the face, and of the
yellow-whiteness of his hair, like snow washed
with gold. I could not reach Coniston in time
to see it, for we were busy at Keswick preparing
a pall to be laid upon the coffin. It was just
such a pall as we knew he would have wished
for. He much disliked the gloom of ordinary
funeral trappings. He had had his own
mother's coffin painted sky-blue, in protest
against prevailing custom, when, in the quiet
Shirley churchyard, he laid to earth " the
dearest earth " he knew. So we designed a
pall of simple unbleached linen, spun by hand
and woven by hand under the eyes of a true
disciple of the Master, who had been the first
for his sake to revive spinning as a home
industry in the dales. We had that pall lined
with the richest, rosiest silk we could obtain,
and on the surface of the pall were sprinkled by
swift embroiderers the wild rose—his favourite

flower—in bud, full bloom, or in shredded petal. At the centre was embroidered a fair wreath of these same flowers of St. George. Within the wild-rose wreath were written, by craft of the needle, the words "Unto this last," and beneath, bordered with gold thread, the initials J. R. It was fitting that this offering should come from members of the Keswick School of Industrial Arts and the Ruskin Linen Industry. These simple experiments of how to bring together joy and beauty in labour of the hands had been inspired by Ruskin's teaching and carried on in the Master's spirit.

The whole Lake Country had been deluged with rain all the week—the winds had moaned among the hills; but Thursday morning broke in silence, and I heard the first thrush sing, and saw the first snowdrop peep from underground. Yet, as one went towards Coniston, the brooks were brimming full, and when I stood upon the hill-crest above Monk Coniston, though Coniston Old Man and Wetherlam were hidden in dense cloud, voices spake from out of the cloud, and the foaming ghyll of Tilberthwaite seemed at that distance across Yewdale almost audible. Wordsworth's lines—

"Loud is the Vale! the voice is up
Wherewith she speaks when storms are gone,"

were constantly ringing up to mind, but as one
gazed down into the deep mountain-trough
wherein the village lay, backed by the russet
and black wall of the Long Crags, though "sad
and even to pain deprest," one could not help
recalling the last two verses of that poem :

> " A power is passing from the earth,
>   To breathless nature's dark abyss ;
> But when the great and good depart,
>   What is it more than this—

> That man who is from God sent forth
>   Doth yet again to God return ?
> Such ebb and flow must ever be,
>   Then wherefore should we mourn ? "

It was not only Wordsworth's poem that was

> " The Comforter who found me there
>   Upon the lonely road,"

for as I gazed over that mere of the Norse
chieftain Thorstein, who gave it his name, there
was suddenly an opening in the clouds. The
south-west was wondrously filled with radiance,
and a burst of glorious sunshine fell upon
Walney Scar and the lowlands of Torver, and,
travelling across the water-flood, seemed to rest
upon the Brantwood slopes with tenderest
benison.

I thought of the times I had seen the Master
there—how, with both arms outstretched, and

cheery silver voice and happy welcome of
blue-gray eyes, he had led me through the
door to his sanctum for earnest talk, or taken
me to his treasure-chamber and shown me
wonder of mineral, glory of drawing, riches
of manuscript illumination, or called me to go
up by winding path through garden woodland
to the Fell.

I remembered how, in his later time of
broken health, I had seen him burdened with
sadness and imaginary woe unutterable and
almost beyond bearing for anguish, by the
thought of a life wasted and work useless and
undone.   I remembered a later visit when I
found him in absolute serenity of unclouded
heart, at rest and in peace, sitting with gentle
hands clasped gazing with love and wonder—
almost as a child might gaze—upon the bouquet
of wild flowers just placed before him for his
pleasure and delight.   " Flowers," he once
wrote, " seem intended for the solace of ordinary
humanity."   He spoke of them then in his full
strength ; he little knew how much they would
mean of help and comfort to his last few years
of painless weakening and failing vigour.

I never went to Brantwood again.   I saw
him sitting there, his long white beard falling
downward as it is seen in that admirable por-

trait which Holman Hunt arranged for Hollyer
to take, and I felt that I should not care to
chance any sight of his enfeebled age, less

"serene and bright
And lovely as a Lapland night,"

that was leading him to the grave. What was
the charm of the visit to Brantwood, for all his
guests, in the time of his health and strength?
It was assuredly this, that the Master of the
house set himself to the task of entertainment,
heart and soul ; added honour to honour by the
way in which he evidently devoted himself un-
sparingly to the visitor. Here was the busiest
man in the literary world of our England giving
precious time to the invited guest, and the guest
knew that in order to do this the giver had risen
earlier from bed that day, and seen "the rose of
morning" blossom and fade upon the Coniston
fell, that he might the better spend hours of the
afternoon as host and entertainer.

Now down below me lay the white village
and the little grey church, with its flag at
half-mast high, and I knew that the Master of
Brantwood had left his home beneath the hills
for ever, and that he lay now within the chancel
swathed in flowers he could not see, waiting in
solemn silence for his burial.

But it was not of Ruskin at Brantwood I

thought most but of Ruskin in the full, breezy vigour of his masterhood, there at the city of his love, that city whose chief shame to-day is that she ever allowed the name of her benefactor and faithfullest servant to be taken from her roll of professors, even though he left her in disdain.   Ruskin at Oxford during his first term of Slade Professorship was the Ruskin I had in mind as I went downward to the valley of his sepulture.

Who can forget those lectures in the museum? —the crowd of expectant students drawn by one magnet from such different pursuits and various lines of study and interest.   His manner of speech had a peculiar power of appeal in it. Its tone and timbre were full of feeling.   It was the speech of one who sang rather than spoke to us.   His message was rhythmic and musical. His peculiar dwelling on and roll of the *r* in such a word as "entirely" was never to be forgotten.   His manner changed with his feeling, and was swift or slow as suited his subject.   He used his hands to emphasize what he said— hands so delicate, so full of expression; hands he used to clap with pleasure, or fold together almost as in prayer.   He won all our hearts, not only by his unconventionality and undonnish ways, but because he took such infinite pains for us; and of all men I ever met he was the best listener. It astonished us young Balliol undergraduates, who were fortnightly guests at his "Hinksey Diggers" breakfast in his rooms at Corpus College, to find not only that he gave us his time but his most serious attention also. Delightful as it was to see him hard at work upon the heap of stones by the wayside of the village green, diligently showing us the right way to break stones, it was more delightful still to be able to stroll back through the sunset meadows and the cool shadowy walks at eventide, and hear him talk of his hopes for Oxford when men should use their muscles less for mere joy of rivalry on river or on the running-path, and more for the service of the poor who lived round about them. People laughed at us and mocked at the Professor, but I do not think there would have been any university settlement in London but for the Hinksey Digging; and most of us who went with the Master to our weekly task of road-making and road-mending have lived to see the lesson which we learned there bear fruit in other such experiments.

People ask me what he looked like. The notable personal features were his delicate aquiline nose, his sensitive mouth, his tender blue eyes, his abundance of straight yellow-brown hair. Below the average height and somewhat hollow-chested, he made up for a certain unrobustness of appearance by his habit of dressing in the thick grey Laxey cloth, as seen in that best of photographs by Barraud. The sky-blue tie, except when he mourned for his mother, was always part of his dress, and a long, delicate gold chain for his watch hung loosely round his neck and fell about his waistcoat.

He has no need to tell the hours any more; we are bound to his burial. As I entered the village and passed to the church, I found the yeomen and dales-folk in their decent black, all going the same way.

"Well, well, we cuddn't deä otherwise but see the last o' th' ald Professor," they said. "He was sic a partic'ler man for th' daale, was so fond o' the bairns an' aw, and when he was stirrin' aboot, for aw that he was much resigned to his oan company, he was nivver abuv passin' time o' daay, and hevin' a crack wi' anybody." What he had been to Coniston let a paragraph from a local paper tell:

"Mr. Ruskin's connection with Coniston practically dates from 1871, when he purchased Brantwood. During the earliest years of his

residence there he was a familiar figure in the
village, and on his way to and from his home
would often step into some wayside cottage and
chat with its inmates.

" He took much interest in the schools, of
which he was one of the managers, and was a
frequent visitor there. At these times he would
enter into pleasant conversation with the scholars,
asking them all sorts of unexpected questions on
a variety of subjects, which, being somewhat out
of the usual range of ordinary school-teaching,
were apt to produce considerable confusion
amongst the youngsters.

" On one occasion he held up a sovereign and
inquired as to the meaning of the words forming
the superscription. Meeting with no response,
he proceeded to explain the matter in charming
fashion, and wound up the lesson by handing
over the coin to the schoolmaster to be expended
amongst his hearers in sweets and chocolate.
He clothed the wall of the school-room with a
large number of *facsimile* drawings, after Prout,
Nash, and others, of famous specimens of architecture, and these are still to be seen there. In
the school yard may also be seen the remains of
a large orrery, which, at considerable expense,
he caused to be constructed for astronomical
instruction, and showing inside its circumference

the principal constellations of the heavens. Or, making his way into the infants' department, he would pick up any of the tiny scholars whom he found to be in trouble, entering into their childish woes with the utmost tenderness, and generally succeeded by some means or other in restoring the smiles to their faces.

"Years before the days of general technical instruction he was the means of establishing a class for wood-carving in Coniston, which continues to exist.

"He took a great interest in the Coniston Institute, and, as the nucleus of a future museum in connection with it, presented a valuable collection of mineralogical specimens. A splendid model of the 'Old Man' mountain and the adjacent hills, constructed for him by Mr. Collingwood, was also handed over to the Institute by him.

"On one occasion only, we believe, did he make any public utterance in Coniston, and this was in connection with a series of lectures organised by the Institute committee probably about twenty years ago. To this he contributed a lecture of a biographical character, dealing with the life of a Lieutenant Edwards, the hero of a minor war on the north-west frontier of India. The lecture attracted a considerable

IN CONISTON CHURCH, BEFORE THE FUNERAL. From Photo. by Walmsley.

number of hearers from various parts of the country.

"Mr. Ruskin's generous assistance in connection with the movement for enlarging the Institute is of more recent date. To him, to the Severns, and to Mr. Collingwood, all associated with Brantwood, may be ascribed the greater part of the credit of providing the village with an Institute such as is possessed by few places of much greater size. The most attractive feature of the novel picture exhibition and sale organised in 1896 for the purpose of adding to the building fund was the inclusion of a large number of signed drawings and sketches by Mr. Ruskin, which alone produced considerably over £100. The greater portion of these were secured by Conistonians, and are now amongst their most cherished possessions.

"It is now a good many years since the Professor, through failing health, ceased to visit the village, although until a comparatively recent time he might be seen taking his favourite walk in the secluded lanes near Brantwood. His last appearance in the village was on the evening of the 7th of April, 1893, when he was present at a concert given by the Coniston Choral Society, at which Mrs. and Miss Severn were among the performers.

"The story of Mr. Ruskin's happy friendship with 'The Ladies of the Thwaite,' Miss Susie Beever and her sister Mary, is well known. To it we are indebted for that delightful collection of letters from his pen which form the volume known as *Hortus Inclusus* as well as the series of extracts from *Modern Painters* which fill the pages of *Frondes Agrestes*. It is a fitting sequel to such a friendship that the dead professor should at last be laid to rest in close proximity to their graves. Conistonians have always been proud that so eminent a man should have made his home amongst them. But their pride and admiration of his wonderful talents have not been their only feelings."

I entered the church, a little homely building with no pretensions, and there before me, filling, as it seemed, the entrance to the tiny chancel, lay a mound of flowers flanked by six large burning candles. This was the "lying in state" we had heard of, and very simple state it seemed. The coffin was hid from view on all sides by the wreaths of floral tributes of friends. Mrs. Severn's cross of tea-roses lay upon it. The children's cross of violets and lilies hid all but the nameplate from view. Mr. Ruskin's friend and biographer, Mr. Collingwood, was in charge, and when the last of the long crowd of solemn fellside faces had passed back from the chancel, the candles were removed, the flowers were taken off, and the rose-embroidered linen pall from Keswick was spread over the coffin. Then two wreaths, and two only, were placed upon the pall—one of camellias, white and red, from the Princess Louise, the other a slender wreath of Italian laurel from his dear old friend Watts, the painter, " For the last of his friends," with the touching direction, " To be placed at his feet." And so we waited for the service.

Meanwhile one had to console the clerk, who had been misled by the fact that the Princess's wreath had come on her Majesty's service from Windsor, and who had supposed it a gift from the Queen. "You see, sir," he said, " there's so many folk asking questions, one gets fairly 'maizled.' I've told the gentlemen o' the papers that the Dean of Christchurch is coming, and he isn't, and I've told 'em the Queen has sent a wreath, and she hasn't, and the paper gentlemen are gone away wid a pack o' lies—oh dear! oh dear!"

It was in keeping with our Northern love of truth that he should be distressed, but I consoled him by the thought that the Queen, as mother of the Princess, had in a way sent that

wreath, and that though the Dean of Christchurch, Ruskin's old College, could not be both
at Westminster Abbey and here at the same
time, he had sent a representative, and so he,
too, was, in a manner, present.

There were many beautiful wreaths with
tender inscriptions, but my eye fell on one
which seemed to have character and originality
about it : " There was a man sent from God,
whose name was John." It was a gift from the
village tailor, and was meant in all deep earnestness to express the thought uppermost in the
heart of a true disciple. It may have seemed
at first sight to lack a little of the sense of
humour, but, in all seriousness, the tailor was
right; if ever man had been a voice crying in
the wilderness, "Prepare ye the way of the
Lord," that man had been John Ruskin.

The service was simple and impressive. The
special hymn I had written, in loving memory of
one to whom I owe so much, was taken up with
heart. Miss Wakefield, an old friend of the
Professor, sang the song, "Comes at times a
stillness as of even," and sang it with all her
soul. And one of Ruskin's friends, son of the
painter Richmond, read very impressively the
lesson. Then the pall-bearers advanced, took
the pall from the altar where it had been

temporarily placed in order that all the con-
gregation might see the Master's simple coffin,
and, replacing the wreath of the Princess and
the painter, they followed the coffin swathed in
its rose embroidery away into the gray light of
the solemn afternoon. Away through the gusts
and the slight rain-sprinkle to the corner of the
churchyard they went, bearing the dead Master
to where his friends for so many years, the
ladies of the Thwaite, the Misses Beever, were
laid before him. When I last saw the coffin in
in its white-lined cell, it was covered with the
rose-red silk of the underlining of the pall. It
seemed to me as if all Oxford had shed its
masters' hoods upon him in token of honour, as
there he lay in his last resting-place.

As I turned away from the grave, I noted
that all about it were growing pines and
deodars, and I remember how he had written
that "the first thing as an event in his life"
that he remembered was "the being taken by
his nurse to the brow of Friar's Crag on
Derwentwater"; and how he had left it on
record that the mossy roots of the Scotch firs
that clasp that crag with their crooked hands
had given him "intense joy, mingled with awe,"
that had associated itself in his mind with all
twining roots of trees ever since.

He was now laid at the foot of the kind tree he had so loved and honoured in his life by the observation and marvellous description. It seemed fitting that the roots of such trees should weave themselves about his sleep, and take his dust to their tender keeping.

CHAPTER IX.

THE UNVEILING OF THE RUSKIN MEMORIAL

AT FRIARS CRAG, KESWICK, OCTOBER 6TH, 1900.

THE weather had for the past fourteen days been alternate shine and shower, but it seemed as if on this particular day the heavens had conspired to do the unveiling without the hand of man; nothing but careful lashing of the linen cover that hid the medallion from view upon its Borrowdale monolith prevented it being blown into ribands.

The fury of the gale had abated about noon, but the men who drove their sheep and cattle from the quagmire of the October Fair-field near Greta bridge, said, "Cooarse wedder! It's not ower yit. We'll happen have a bit of wind afore neet."

They were right. At two o'clock the cloud wrack descended upon the hills and shut out

Borrowdale from sight.   Then with the roar
of the equinox the gale swept down the New-
lands vale upon the lake, and Derwentwater
rose like an angry sea and all its white-maned
horses came at a gallop to Friars Crag.   With
great difficulty the boat which was coming
from the Island with Mrs. Severn to perform
the unveiling ceremony made the Duke of
Portland's boathouse, and as we joined the
brave disciples of Ruskin who had determined,
fair or foul, no weather should keep them from
this act of honour to their teacher and their
friend, it seemed as if what with the noise of
the wind in the tree tops and the sound of
the waves upon the shore, little or nothing
would be heard of the addresses that were
about to be delivered.

But what a fine sight it was, that sea from
the south-west.   The hills now looming, now
lost in cloud wrack—the ancient fir trees
through whose mossy roots Ruskin as a little
child had gazed with such joy and awe upon
the dark water below, loud with storm.

Somehow or other one felt that the scene
had gained even by all this 'business of the
elements' a kind of grandeur for the occasion;
and as if the very storm-gods themselves,
whose work and being Ruskin had painted

JOHN·RUSKIN·

·MDCCCXIX·+·MDCCC·

·THE·FIRST·THING·
WHICH·I·REMEMBER·
AS·AN·EVENT·IN·LIFE·
WAS·BEING·TAKEN·BY·
MY·NURSE·TO·THE·BROW·
OF·FRIAR'S·CRAG·ON·
DERWENTWATER·

From Photo. by Abraham.

THE RUSKIN MEMORIAL AT FRIAR'S CRAG, KESWICK,

in such graphic words, were coming together to do the dead man reverence.

Arrived at the spot we found the children and their teachers ready to sing the special hymn that had been written for the Master's funeral, and those who had assembled very willingly came with them from the crag top into shelter on its lee side. There, though the gale blew the words away, they sang that solemn hymn as only children could, and after the hymn, Mrs. Severn very bravely delivered the following short address :

" Ladies and Gentlemen and Children : I feel honoured in having been asked by Canon Rawnsley to unveil this memorial to my beloved cousin, John Ruskin.

" You all know, I believe, that it was on this spot as a child that there was created in his mind an enthusiasm for nature that lasted to the end of his life. It was a curious coincidence that only a few weeks before he left us I read him aloud Edna Lyall's ' Hope the Hermit,' which brought back vividly the scenes surrounding us now, that he loved so dearly in childhood.

" It was also in Keswick that his delight in mineralogy began and the first specimens of his collection were got. In middle life (as he is so well and appropriately represented in this beautiful medallion) he came again here, and wrote letters to his mother and me daily, rapturous in his admiration of Derwentwater.   The outlines of trees seen against sky or lake had always a peculiar charm for him.

"On my first walk with him on a lovely April day at his Denmark Hill home, he surprised me by saying, 'Put your head down and look at those tree branches against the sky.'   It was a revelation to me.   Later, when recovering from dangerous illness at Matlock Bath, while I was left alone, almost expecting he would never wake, he said, 'Open the window wide, and let me see the trees against the sky.'

"It was a few days after he said, 'If only I could lie down in Coniston water I should get well.'   Within a month Brantwood was offered to him, and when he accepted it I showed surprise at his rashness in buying a place without ever seeing it.   He said eagerly, 'My dear child, any place opposite Coniston Old Man *must* be beautiful,' and to the end, thank God, it was so to him, whether he sat at his study chair or looked from his bed, and he now rests in the shadow of it at sunset.

"This interesting monument will, I trust, help to keep his memory dear in the hearts of all whom he taught to see what was beautiful in nature, and good in their lives."

The storm seemed almost to grow in sound and fury. The wild wood voices of the firs and oaks drowned human speech. But we could not help saying, even to the wind and the rain as they swept by, some few words of the reason we had met in such a storm to do homage to one who is far beyond all storm, in the haven where he would be. The following, or so much as was audible in that great whirlwind of sound, were the words in which I tried to explain the object of the meeting :

" We meet to-day to honour the memory of the last great poet of the English Lakes. For Ruskin was a poet as well as a prophet, and though he wrote for the most part in prose and not in rhyme, his choice of words and his sense of rhythm and sound, his fine balance of sentence, his inevitable ear, brought it about that his prose was always noblest poesy.

" We meet to-day to honour the memory not only of an artist and an art critic, but of an idealist who was also a social reformer. I remember his once saying to me, ' Rawnsley, when men have forgotten every word of my *Modern Painters*, they will think about my *Crown of Wild Olive* and *Unto This Last*.

It was for this reason that when loyal hands and loving hearts here in Keswick embroidered the covering of the handspun linen for the Master's coffin, the words 'Unto This Last' were written by the needle in the midst of the crown of wild roses upon the pall. It is for this reason that we have taken care to see that the crown of wild olive shall be by the hands of the sculptor and bronze caster set as background to the portrait profile unveiled to-day.

"We meet to-day to honour the worker's friend, the man who more than others of his time so believed in the possibilities of a happier life for the working men, that he set himself against traditions and the ordinary accepted theories of capital and labour, and even as he bade the artist know that all great art was prose, he bade the worker know that all true work was joy. If ever our sulphurous-smoke-smothered cities of the plain see blue sky above their heads, if ever our factory-plagued-and-poisoned rivers run clear, if ever plant life, and tree life, and bird life return to cheer the toiler in the towns, we shall owe it largely to the spirit of the man who perceived and taught that all good work might be worship, and was meant for joy, and that no good work was possible until a man had ceased to be a hand, a mere machine, a cog in an iron wheel, and had been allowed to bring his mind and soul to the task, under conditions that admitted of happiness and health.

"We meet to-day to honour a man who taught as Dante taught, as Wordsworth taught, the harmony of things, the unity of the Divine purpose, and who did all he could to call us back to Nature and to God.

"We meet to-day to think of one who, as he taught others to do, trusted in the living God,— the Father Almighty, Maker of Heaven and earth, and in the kindness of His Law; who trusted in the nobleness of human nature, in the majesty of its faculties, the fulness of its mercy, and the joy of its love ; who knew the worth of time, and wasted nothing of his working day ; who, whatever his hands found to do, did it with all his might, and set upon his seal the word 'To-day'; who would not deceive nor injure any living being for gain or pleasure, and ever preached and practised the knightliness of old ; who would not kill or harm any living thing needlessly, nor destroy any beautiful thing ; who strove to comfort all gentle life and to guard and perfect all natural beauty upon earth ; who strove to raise his own body and soul daily unto higher power of duty and happiness, not in rivalry or contention with others, but for the help and delight and honour of others and for the joy and peace that comes of service.

"This is the man we meet to honour, a man who with all the gladness that came to him from his generosity, all the triumph that was his from excellence in workmanship, all the peace that love of Nature and perception of beauty gave him, was nevertheless a man of many sorrows and much disappointment.

"This is the man we meet to honour, the tireless teacher, the self-sacrificing friend. A man who with desire for life that he might minister to the life of the nation, saw very little of the travail of his soul, but loving not his own life unto the death, wore himself out in the helping of his fellows.

"This is the man we meet to honour, a man who yearning for sympathy found it not till the day for sympathy had almost gone by, and whose health was so broken in his latter years that he scarce could realise how much the gospel that he preached was prevailing and would prevail.

"This is the man who added to our powers of perception, and sympathy as a nation; who quickened morality in the affairs of men. The man who not only by thought and diction has permanently enriched our English literature, but has bequeathed to us the legacy of a great example of service and the gift of a pure spirit that shall not fail."

I dwelt for a moment on Ruskin's special connection with Keswick and Derwentwater, and after a word of thanks to Mrs. Severn, to whose affectionate and tender care of her cousin in his declining years all lovers of Ruskin owe so much, briefly described the monument as follows :

" The monument that we unveil to-day, consists of a simple monolithic block of Borrowdale stone, rough and unhewn as it came from the quarry. It is of the type of the standing stones of Galloway, which are the earliest Christian monuments of the Celtic people now extant. This form has been chosen as linking us here with that land across the Solway, whence Ruskin's fore-elders came. Upon one side is incised a simple Chi-Rho, enclosed in a circle after the fashion of those earliest crosses, with the following inscription beneath from *Deucalion*, Lecture xii., par. 40 : ' *The Spirit of God is around you in the air you breathe—His glory in the light that you see, and in the fruitfulness of the earth and the joy of His creatures, He has written for you day by day His revelation, as He has granted you day by day your daily bread.*'

"It may serve to perpetuate to passers by one of the messages of the Teacher, and the cross above it may strike a keynote which, at any rate, I find ringing up from so much that Ruskin wrote, and from all of his daily life I knew or have heard of.

"On the other side of the monolith, facing the lake and the scene which Ruskin once described to a friend of mine 'as one of the three most beautiful scenes in Europe,' we have a medallion in bronze, the careful work of Signor Lucchesi, representing Ruskin not as the old man and invalid of later days, but as he was in his prime, at the time I knew him best, at Oxford, in the early seventies. The head is in profile; a crown of wild olive is seen in the background of the panel, which is dished or hollowed to give the profile high relief, and Ruskin's favourite motto, 'To-day,' is introduced among the olive leaves in the background over the head. Above the portrait is the name 'John Ruskin,' beneath are his dates 1819 to 1900. Beneath these again is incised the inscription, '*The first thing that I remember as an event in life was being taken by my nurse to the brow of Friars Crag, Derwentwater.*'

"The lettering has been designed and drawn by Ruskin's biographer, Mr. Collingwood, and was so designed to indicate that particular dot and dash style of drawing which was a favourite method with the Master. We have to thank Mr. Bromley, the stone cutter, for his care in selecting the block, and his nephew for his cutting of the letters so well.

"The monument in its simplicity and sincerity has at any rate the merit of telling its own story, and of being devoid of any unnecessary ornament. It is of the stone of the country, and placed here on this grassy knoll among the trees, seems to be a natural part of the surroundings, and can in no way, either by colour or by scale, incur the charge of being vulgar or intrusive or a blot upon the scene. It grows out of the ground.

"It is erected by leave of the Lord of the Manor here, in the neighbourhood of a scene so dear and memorable to John Ruskin, in entire accordance with his teaching. He has told us that 'whenever the conduct or writings of any individual have been directed or inspired by Nature, Nature should be entrusted with their monument'; and again, 'that since all monuments to individuals are to a certain extent triumphant, they must not be placed where Nature has no elevation of character.'

"The elevated nature of this scene will not

be called in question. And this simple memorial has been placed by friends and lovers of John Ruskin here to show our gratitude for that servant of God and of the people whose eyes were opened here first to the wonder of creation and the beauty of God's handiwork ; and in the full belief that the scene will lose nothing of natural dignity and power to impress by the memory of how it was able, in the year 1824, to impress and inspire John Ruskin."

A move was now made from our place of shelter to the place where on its grassy knoll among the trees the monolith stood. At a given signal the strings that bound the veil over the face of the medallion were loosed. At the same moment the children broke into a hearty singing of the National Anthem, and the simple but memorable ceremony was at an end. The waves thundered their applause, the very trees of the forest clapped their hands, and we turned away, and left, as we hope, to the care of centuries, this pillar of remembrance to one who owed so much of his heart's first awe and gladness and reverence to the scene at Friars Crag,—who taught so many of his time the wonder of creation, and showed all hearts that could feel, and eyes that would observe, where true joy was to be found.

CHAPTER X.

THE MEMORIAL CROSS AT CONISTON.

As I walked up Yewdale this eventide and heard the stream, that was almost silent in the day, murmuring with increase of sound as the stillness grew, another song was in my ears, for the song of a poet who years ago in happy days of honeymoon, walked the fields and byways of Coniston came back to mind:

> " All along the valley stream that flashest white
> Deepening thy voice with the deepening of the night,
> All along the valley where thy waters flow
> I walked with one I loved two and thirty years ago."

But it was not of Tennyson, nor of Tennyson's friend in the vale of Cauteretz that the Yewdale stream or The White Lady Ghyll was eloquent.

It was true that I could say as I listened by the stream,

"For all along the valley by thy rocky bed
   Thy living voice to me was the voice of the dead,"

but the dead it spoke of to me was the
friend whose dust lay beneath the grass of
the Coniston Churchyard,

"And all along the valley, by rock, and cave, and tree,
   The voice of the dead was a living voice to me."

In truth Ruskin was at my side as I
wandered homeward, the work of his laborious day had come freshly to mind. I had
been to see the beautiful Memorial Cross that
had been erected by his friends the Severns
over his last resting-place. And it was through
that cross and its careful sculpturing that more
than ever 'the voice of the dead was a living
voice to me.'

Others will go to Coniston Churchyard and
read the story of Ruskin's life-work as told by
the grey-green monolith ; let me describe it :

It is clear at a glance that the designer,
Mr. Collingwood, has had in his mind the
early Anglian crosses of Bewcastle, Rothwell
and Irton. That is to say, that the Hammer
of Thor which in Anglian times still asserted
itself, and not the Crown of glory, the
Nimbus about the head of Christ, has been
adapted as the cross head. And this is fitting,

for the churchyard lies in the valley of Thors-stein of the Mere — the Thurston water of our day. So the Anglian hammer and not the wheel-head has been chosen for the head of the cross. To be in keeping with those old days of sun worship, on the western head of the cross and on the outside of the hammer head has been engraved the 'svastica' or sun-worship sign. While to show that this cross is the sign of Him Who came to be the Sun for all the world—One with the Father and the Holy Spirit, there is sculptured on the eastern side of the cross-head the boss that may mean both sun and world, and round it is an interlacing pattern that with triple plait may signify, as the 'Triquatra' does in other parts of the cross stem, the Blessed and Undivided Trinity.

Those who come to see the cross will notice that the shaft, which appears to rise about nine feet from the ground, stands also on a triple step or base we call a Calvary, so that one cannot help being reminded that the way of the Cross was the way he tried to tread whose life of self-sacrifice closed at Brantwood in the spring of 1900.

All will be impressed with the colour of the stone as harmonising with the surroundings.

Viewed either against the dark 'deodars' or
the yew tree and the distant slope of Coniston
Old Man, the cross seems to be what it
indeed is, a natural part of the scene. For
the stone—volcanic ash that was showered
out upon the land from the volcano at Bowfell long before the Alps were dreamed of—
came from Mossrigg quarry at Tilberthwaite—
that Tilberthwaite beloved of Ruskin—and
Elterwater supplied the stone for the base.
Beautiful in the sunshine, it is more beautiful
after rain, for then the moss agate greenness
of the stone comes out. Purest silica as it
is, no weathering will ever blunt or blur the
finest or tenderest strokes of the sculptor's
chisel upon it.

It was a happy thought that bade Mr.
Collingwood select the stone from the land
his master loved so well; it was a happier
that he induced a stone-cutter, Miles of Ulver-
ston, who had done work for Mr. Ruskin in
the old days, to undertake the task of sculpturing the design he had prepared. Nothing
could have been more consonant with the
wishes of the 'Master' than that his friend and
biographer should be the designer of the
memorial. And Mr. Collingwood, when he was
casting about for the shape of the memorial,

did well to remember how deeply interested Ruskin had in his later years become in all the runic crosses of the North.

Now let us read this Bible of Coniston, this work of remembrance of Ruskin's life-work, as written for us in imperishable stone.

As a lad Ruskin delighted in rhyme and its making. Here then at the base of the eastern side of the cross sits beneath the olive branch with the bay tree growing in front of him a lad with a seven-stringed lyre. Above him, as emblematical of the intricacy of life and the many influences which moulded his to fair purpose—father, mother, teacher, travel, Oxford, art, poetry, books and fields and the love of them—may be seen the tangled knot-work found so often upon Celtic monuments, and known in almost all the early ornamental art of the world. Above this is a panel with the name in plain lettering, 'John Ruskin,' and below it the dates, 1819, 1900, divided by the 'Svastica,' to show what days were lived beneath the sun. Above this is more tangle of knot-work and in a panel above, the boy-poet is seen now to be the young artist. Flowers that he loved are at his feet, pine trees he loved are in the background as he sits at his sketching, and, over all, the great sun rises,

that 'Rose of Morning' he had so often
seen upon the Coniston fells. I suppose we
must look on this panel as telling us that
Ruskin was the author of *Modern Painters*.

But the artist grows up, goes to Venice
and his next work, his book, the *Stones of
Venice*, is typified by the Lion of St. Mark
in a panel whose outside rim runs on and
connects itself with the uppermost panel of
all. Therein we see the seven-branched
candlestick of the Revelation,—the seven-
branched candlestick of the Tabernacle of the
Jews, signifying to us that crowning work of
Ruskin's earlier life, *The Seven Lamps of
Architecture*.

Now the first chapter of his life is closed.
The tale of the first forty years of his life
is ended, with all he wrought and taught and
thought about. But its history, its principles,
its meaning, its ethics has been pictured for
us on the eastern face of the cross. Let us
go to the western side and read upon this
Bible of Coniston a record of the work he
wrought and thought and taught and fought
for in the domain of life and labour,—its aim,
its possibilities, its duties and its joy. On
this eastern side we have had record of Ruskin
as poet, artist and writer of the beautiful in

THE GRAVES OF JOHN RUSKIN AND THE LADIES OF THE THWAITE.

Art and Nature; on the western side we find
in five panels the story of Ruskin the social
reformer writ clear in pictorial rune. The
lowest panel tells us of the parable of Christ
and the labourers in the vineyard. The un-
generous and dissatisfied worker stands on
Christ's left hand, the grateful, and uncomplain-
ing on His right; above their heads is seen
the vine and the vine-leaves spread with grace
and beauty, and fill the spaces between this
lower panel and the next above it. "Friend,
I do thee no wrong," the words are seen in
the face of the gentle and the just Jesus
Christ. "Take that thine is and go thy way.
I will give unto this last even as unto thee."
We remember Ruskin's *Unto this Last* as
we gaze.

The next book that Ruskin gave the world
after his *Unto this Last* was *Sesame and
Lilies*, and the designer has signified this by
lilies surrounded by a cloud of tiny pellets
which may mean, as he tells us in his interesting
monograph, the little cakes of honey, or flour
and honey,—the sugar plums that stood for
Sesame in Greek times. I confess to thinking
that there should have been some little scroll
with "This is sesame" writ upon it, for the
casual observer will take the pellets to be

P

not sugar plums, but pollen-dust, shed abroad
from the Virgin's lilies in the roundel.

Next, and occupying the central and most
important part of the shaft, with angel heads
supporting the panel, is seen a fair crowned
queenly figure winged, holding in her right
hand a key and a nail, and leaning her left
hand upon a club.   This can be no other
than *Fors Clavigera*, Fors with her club for
strength and deed, Fors with her key for
strength and patience, Fors with her nail
for strength and labour, such nails as only
masters of assemblies hold.   Here, then, pictured for all who run to read, is set before
us the work to which Ruskin devoted the
latter part of his life.   The work he felt was
the best he did.   Work done for the workers
of Britain and the world who by patience
and by law should become doers of worthy
deeds to the honour of God and the helping
of their brothers unto right.

In the panel above, is seen a crown of
wild olive whose binding riband is the endless knot of Mystery.   The lectures Ruskin
gave on Work and Traffic and War had as
the strand that bound them all together
Ruskin's thoughts on the mystery and deep
significance of life, and it is this that the

designer has had in mind as he drew the knot-work for this panel. Above, and highest of all in the cross shaft, is set Ruskin's favourite sign, St. George and the Dragon.

The designer did right to set this picture of St. George and the Dragon in the shaft, for though the Guild of St. George failed of his intent, it did not fail in shadowing forth the wishes of the master of that guild, nor in proving that scattered up and down the land were men who could at a call rally to the cry St. George for merry England. Who knows but this picture in the Bible of Coniston may yet avail to urge men who are trying to live and work in the spirit of the master of the Guild, to band together and carry on the work whose hope, though it fell short of fulfilment, cheered Ruskin to the end.

We have now read the story of the life-work of John Ruskin as writer and teacher. It remains for us to think of him as a man of many interests and mysterious influence and more mysterious suffering. On the north side of the cross shaft this latter part of the teacher's life has been bodied forth by a long endless band of knot-work ornament whose careful working out is a pleasure to look

upon. And as we think of the sorrow of
the man's life,—its disappointments,—its long
infirmity,—its many interests, his influence
so world-wide, apparently so unending, shines
through it all, and we thank God that it was
our privilege to have known him and learned
of him.

It is with a sense of joy that, leaving the
sunless-side of the cross for the southern side,
we there find ourselves in presence of a
scroll of Ruskin's much loved wild rose that
springs upward from base to height. Flowers,
and especially wild flowers of these lakeland
lanes and woods and fells, meant so much to
him, and here is set in bud and bloom and
fruitage the flower that he loved the best;
the flower he chose as emblem for his
workers.

Nor has the designer forgotten how
Ruskin described with exquisite care the ways
of robin, kingfisher and squirrel, and here,—as
may be seen in the scrolls upon the Bewcastle cross,—the squirrel sits and is happy
with his hazel fruit, while in another part of
it the robin watches for his food and the
kingfisher dives for tiny fish. Life and food
and happy content, beauty and song, the
winged hunter of the stream and wild wood

creature is bodied forth for us, that we may know how much of pleasure for this life Ruskin found in study of the ways, not only of men, but of bird and beast also.

So the Bible of Coniston is read through, and we turn away from the grave grateful to designer and sculptor for the memorial set and the pillar of remembrance raised above the Master's sleep.

Of course there will be criticism, even as one gazes one hears a voice saying that cross shafts ought not to be turned into library catalogues ; that all early Anglian crosses, if they admitted figures, only admitted them under conditions of severe treatment ; that it is questionable if the work is simple enough, and the like. For those who come and read the message of the cross such criticism seems to vanish into thin air, and to be heard no more. And yet, where so much is told, one asks for more, and one wonders why it was that to make the story of the life complete there was no suggestion given of Ruskin's love of running streams and lichened rocks, Ruskin the man with the geologist's hammer, and the mineralogist's microscope.

Then, too, one could have wished that it had been possible to set before us Ruskin's work as preacher and prophet to his time. One would have been glad to see the first sermon that he preached, as a child, sculptured on the base of the cross. "People be good! If you are good, God will love you. If you are not good, God will not love you." That was his first sermon, it was his last also.

Criticise how we may, one thing is above criticism. It is the love that dictated the work and the devotion that carried it through, and all who revere Ruskin's memory will feel that designer and sculptor alike deserve our thanks for the honour they have done his resting-place.

I at any rate was glad to have had the Master's life-work so concisely put forth in picture before me, and as I walked homeward through the growing twilight—

"All along the valley, by rock, and cave, and tree,
The voice of the dead was a living voice to me."

MEMORIAL POEMS.

I.

THE MASTER AT REST.

BRANTWOOD, SUNDAY, JANUARY 21ST, 1900.

THE rose of morning fades, and ghostly pale
  The mountains seem to move into the rain ;
  The leafless hedges sigh, the water-plain
Sobs, and a sound of tears is in the Vale ;
For he whose spirit-voice shall never fail,
  Whose soul's arm ne'er shall lifted be in vain
  —God's Knight, at rest beyond the touch of pain,
Lies clad in Death's impenetrable mail.

And all the men whose helmets ever wore
  The wild red-rose St. George for sign has given
    Stand round, and bow the head and feel their swords,
    And swear by him who taught them deeds not words,
To fight for Love, till, as in days of yore
  Labour have joy, and earth be filled with Heaven.

II.

AT RUSKIN'S GRAVE.

ON HIS BIRTHDAY, FEBRUARY 8TH, 1900.

FOR this his natal day the heavens had lent
  Unto his rest their fitting garniture,
  The snow-fall lay so innocently pure
O'er him whose life was pure and innocent ;

One way it seemed the foot-marks all were bent,
As if the mounded earth had magic lure,
And from the grave to cheer and reassure
A spirit voice continually was sent.

The silver mountains called from bluest air,
But he had entered to his prophet's cell
New thought in deeper quietude to take,
While from an unassailable citadel
In holy ground beside the tranquil lake
Came forth his mind to make the world more fair.

III.

AT RUSKIN'S FUNERAL.

Men cry, " There is no open vision now !
From out the land the prophets cease and fail ;
The last great gladiator falls and dies ! "
The hollow winds from off the mountain's brow
Moan, lamentation fills the darkened vale,
And the pale lake is loud with sobs and cries.

Belovéd presence of the field and grove,
Thou heart and guardian-spirit of the scene,
Dost thou at last forsake thy fell and shore ?
Blue eyes so full of tenderness and love,
So swift with scornful hate of all things mean.
Ah, must ye flash your fire, your love, no more ?

There is no yeoman ranging on the hill,
There is no patient fisher by the lake,
No child from school in yonder village near,
But knew of old thy graciousness of will,
But loved his home the better for thy sake,
And felt a single word and look was cheer.

Weep then ! ye simple shepherds of the fell !
  Yours is a cause of grieving for the world !
    The earth weeps with you,—rocks, and trees, and flowers !
In fair Savoy I hear the funeral knell,
  Half-mast the flags in Venice are unfurled,
    Sad Florence mourns from all her purple towers.

Lo ! with the shepherd sons, are mourners here—
  The man who caught the spirit of the sky,
    And made his canvas speak to heart and soul,—
Grave Wordsworth, he who saw thy promise clear,—
  Grim Carlyle, one in arms and chivalry,
    And that young Prince who sooner reached his goal.

One [1] spirit comes from far across the main,
  Leaving the shy, sequestered Harvard cell,
    Who gave his friend new heart in days of old
To dare the perilous paths of right again ;
  With that young Oxford scholar loved so well. [2]
    Who laid down life for poor men of Christ's fold.

He [3] too from Oxford—fine locks flowing grey,
  Who walked the halls of learning and of youth,
    Close at his side, a dear familiar friend.
And one [4] who high above the Barmouth bay
  Gave to the master for St. George's truth
    The fisher homes her love and care could tend.

One seemed to stand in sadness, still unbent
  By weight of years, and still undimmed of eye,
    The poet-painter, [5] he whose heart had come
With that green crown of fadeless laurel, sent
  For his last friend,—frail child of Italy,
    Nursed for such service in his Surrey home.

---

[1] Charles E. Norton.   [2] Arnold Toynbee.   [3] Sir H. Acland.
[4] Mrs. Talbot.   [5] G. F. Watts, R.A.

These mingle with us, but one household guest
    Moves shaggy-browed, hawk-eyed, to join the throng—
        An honest merchant, with the wife who bore
Her son to honour ; these have left their rest—
    The Shirley grave—where they have waited long
        To give sweet welcome to that further shore.

And I might see her face our sorrow share,
    Who told by pencilled line and printed page
        The peasant joys and pain of Tuscan wilds ;[1]
And they whose gentle tutelary care
    Were long the solace of his faltering age,
        Whose children kept the sage's heart a child's.[2]

Ah ! yes, but other guests to-day have come,
    And in their hands St. George's rose they bring—
        Men sworn by all their master taught and wrought
To bring back honour to her ancient home,
    To make earth once again for gladness sing
        And build for nobler life with nobler thought.

There is no eye but seems a moment dim,
    No heart but feels as if it, too, must break,
        The spell of all the poet-preacher knew
Has so possessed the souls that yearn for him,
    For he it was who came hard hearts to make
        Tender, and win by sympathy the true.

But as we stand beneath the mountain lawn
    That filled his morn so oft with praise and prayer,
        From out the grave there comes a solemn voice
" Quit you like men ! for in whatever dawn
    He lives and moves who found earth's dawn so fair,
        His soul has rest,"—and hearing, we rejoice.

[1] Miss Alexander.   [2] The Arthur Severns.

In Loving Memory, Coniston, January 25th, 1900.

" Knowest thou that the Lord will take away thy master from thy head to-day ? And he said, Yea, I know it."

THE prophets cease from out the land,
    The counsellors are gone,
The lips to kindle and command
    Are silent one by one.

Our master taken from our head,
    In sorrow, here we pray—
' Lord, teach us in his steps to tread ;
    Be Thou our guide and stay,

Till all the righteousness he loved,
    The sympathy he sought,
The truth by deed and word he proved,
    Be made our daily thought.'

He gave us eyes, for we were blind ;
    He bade us know and hear ;
By him the wonder of the mind
    Of God on earth was clear.

We knew the travail of his soul,
    We thank Thee for his rest ;
Lord, lead us upward to his goal—
    The pure, the true, the best !

                        AMEN.

EVENING AND MORNING.

WORDS by the Rev. GREGORY SMITH. MUSIC by
              Sir H. S. OAKELEY.

COMES at times, a stillness as of even,
    Steeping the soul in memories of love,

As when the glow is sinking out of heaven,
  As when the twilight deepens in the grove.

Comes at length, a sound of many voices,
  As when the waves break lightly on the shore ;
As when at dawn the feathered choir rejoices,
  Singing aloud because the night is o'er.

Comes at times, a voice of days departed,
  On the dying breath of evening borne,
Sinks then the trav'ller, faint and weary-hearted,
  " Long is the way," it whispers, "and forlorn."

Comes at last, a voice of thrilling gladness,
  Borne on the breezes of the rising day ;
Saying, "The Lord shall make an end of sadness,"
  Saying, "The Lord shall wipe all tears away."

INDEX

For EU product safety concerns, contact us at Calle de José Abascal, 56–1°,
28003 Madrid, Spain or eugpsr@cambridge.org.